What p(
THE GIFT CALLED .P

My friend Barry E. Knight puts his heart into words in *The Gift Called Leadership*. His life's journey entwined by intersections with other leaders creates a rich tapestry where you will find yourself. Indeed, leadership is a gift.

—*Sam Chand*
Leadership Consultant, Author of Leadership Pain

The Gift Called Leadership isn't just a book; it's a roadmap for cultivating leaders who lead with purpose, compassion, and integrity. It was an honor to have Barry demonstrate the principles in this book for two years as he trained our police officers on community engagement. I am confident this book will empower individuals to become the leaders our world desperately needs.

—*Chief Larry Gonzalez*
Riverside Police Department, Riverside, CA

Barry nailed it. The impact of leadership, specifically a leader's 'presence' and how they empower others to succeed cannot be understated. Leadership is about empowering those we are privileged to lead and creating an environment where those self-directed, empowered team members grow, thrive, and succeed. We have had Barry speak to our leaders regarding this topic. His passion and purposeful action plan continue to inspire us to achieve greater levels of success and this book is another great resource to help lead and achieve. I strongly recommend *The Gift Called Leadership: How the Leader's 'Presence' Empowers Others to Succeed* to anyone wanting to take their team to the next level.

—*Shawn Mandel*
Vice President, Waste Connections, Inc.

y E. Knight does it again as he brings to clarity what
ntional leadership does for an individual and an orga-
ation. The choice of words, clear examples, and level of
sponsibility motivates me as an experienced leader to do
ven more to inspire others and build trust. Once you know,
then you grow. One's calling is not complete until you are
impacting others. Barry shows the way.

—Dr. Judy D. White
Retired Superintendent, Riverside County Office of Education
Founder and President, Mosaic Legacy

Barry's book is as powerful as his speaking. As I read
each sentence, I heard his pauses, articulation, and powerful delivery. Everything Barry does is done so with a
'purpose-driven agenda.' He values everyone's time and
ensures that readers will receive value from the beginning
of the book through the last word written. He has once again
'knocked it out of the park'!

—Bobby Spiegel
CEO, President, CORONA Chamber

What sets this book apart is its relatability. Whether you're a
seasoned leader or just starting on your leadership journey,
the practical lessons shared here are invaluable. The author's
words resonate deeply, reminding us that leadership isn't
just about authority, but about cultivating trust, fostering
collaboration, and nurturing growth.

—Sam Itani
FACHE, CEO, Corona Regional Medical Center

As a CEO for over twenty-five years, I can say that *The Gift
Called Leadership* is an exceptional body of work that illu-
minates the profound impact of a leader's presence on the
success of those they guide. Through insightful anecdotes

and well-researched analysis, the book brilliantly demonstrates how a leader's mere presence can catalyze growth and achievement within a team. Readers will discover how a leader's authentic presence fosters a culture of collaboration, encouraging individuals to embrace challenges and exceed their expectations.

—*Walter B. Davis, MBA*
President and CEO, Nevada Health Centers

In *The Gift Called Leadership*, Barry E. Knight eloquently describes how we all can step up to be Leaders with a capital L. Read this book and decide if you want to be a "Leader" or "leader." You get to choose!

—*Amy Hiett*
Executive Coach, Co-founder of The Table Group

Leaders who desire to expand their perspectives on effective leadership should get this book. Barry provides many valuable insights on Leadership as a seat for making a positive difference in the lives of people. Those in Leadership positions enable results when they focus on excellence, precision, and attentiveness to create a thriving and impactful environment. Barry leverages clear explanations, inspiring examples, and memorable stories to make his points in support of the reader's growth and development. This book, *The Gift Called Leadership*, should be read by all who want to become a more attentive, growth-oriented, and strategic Leader.

—*Dr. Peter Chee*
President and CEO of ITD World, a leading multinational corporation for Human Resource Development

Cover design by: Mattie Wells
Cover photo by: Andrew van Tilborgh

ISBN: 978-1-960678-97-3   1 2 3 4 5 6 7 8 9 10

Printed in the United States of America

How the Leader's 'Presence'
Empowers Others to Succeed

THE GIFT
— CALLED —
LEADERSHIP

BARRY E. KNIGHT

AVAIL

Dedication

To the Leaders who boldly say 'yes' to the vision, work, and risk of making things remarkably better for others!

CONTENTS

ACKNOWLEDGMENTS

I am so grateful for the remarkable individuals who have blessed my life and journey, providing me with the wisdom, love, and support that I need to do what I am called to do. Your presence and influence have shaped both this book and the man that I am and will become.

To my wife, Sacheen—thank you for giving me the space to commit to my passion and for standing with me through the highs and lows of the journey. I love you with all of my heart. You are God's gift to me!

To my three amazing children, BJ, Charles Edward, and Sydnei Erica—thank you for understanding the late nights and the passionate pursuits. Your presence reminds me of the legacy I strive to leave behind and the world I aim to create for your future.

To my mother-in-love, siblings, and entire family—your love is a reminder that we are part of something larger than ourselves.

To my pastors, Tom and Heather Flores—thank you for praying for me and my family. We are grateful for your ministry.

To Dr. Sam Chand—your wisdom and insights continue to shape my perspective.

To Jeff Van Wagenen—thank you for opening the door to a new season in my life. Your Leadership is guiding me to opportunities I never imagined possible.

To Dr. Judy White (Auntie)—your unwavering belief in the best of me has been a driving force in my life. You selflessly opened a door that literally built the platform on which I now stand, grow, and expand.

To Bishop Ronald C. Hill—a father, spiritual guide, and covering. Your prayers and words of life have been a steady source of strength. Your faith in God empowers me to walk in my purpose with confidence.

To the AVAIL Publishing team—Martijn van Tilborgh, Sarah Petelle, Debbie Chand, and John Schondelmayer—your dedication and expertise brought this book to life. Your commitment to excellence is truly remarkable.

To Mattie Wells—your artistic brilliance and design expertise gave this book a face that resonates with its message. Your work is a masterpiece that speaks volumes.

To Fiorella (Fiore) Contreras—my executive assistant. Your proactive approach and support have been instrumental in shaping and growing our Leadership coaching business. Your attention to detail makes me a better Leader.

To the BEK Impact Co. team and consultants—your collaboration and dedication have been a driving force behind my mission. Together, we impact lives.

To Don Carthorn—your guidance and belief in me propelled me to where I stand today. Your influence has been immeasurable.

To each of you who have walked this path with me, and to those whose names aren't listed but whose impact is etched in my heart—I am deeply grateful. Your belief, love, and encouragement are the fuel that drives me forward.

With sincere gratitude,
Barry E. Knight

— CHAPTER 1 —
AWAKEN THE SPIRIT OF LEADERSHIP

*C*ongratulations! *You worked hard to be the leader in your* organization. But Leadership is more than a title. It is more than just occupying a position of authority. Leadership is not receiving a long-awaited promotion or winning an election. Leadership is a calling. It is an expression of hope that helps others see what else is possible. It is a duty and mandate to make things better for those you lead and serve.

Leadership is a beautiful gift that transforms how people live, work, collaborate, and see the world. As the Leader, you possess something of high value. You have a very costly gift. But this gift is not for you. It's for them. It's for the people you lead and serve. Please note that this book is not about teaching you how to increase profits or strategies to grow and scale your organization. No. This book is about you and how your Leadership moves people to say, "I trust you and I want to follow and achieve great things with you!" Increased profits, growth, and scale are a result of this kind of Leadership.

This requires a total shift in how you think, what you believe, how you speak, and how you show up as a Leader. If you want people to willingly give their time, talent, and resources to making your vision a reality, then you must increase your capacity to inspire, engage, and empower people.

Because of this mandate, Leadership becomes difficult to define. Is it simply influence? Or is it more about creating? Maybe Leadership is being a light in dark places. Or is it being a bridge that opens the way for people to move from what is to what is to come? Ask ten people for their definition of Leadership and you'll get twenty different definitions. Let's not attempt to define Leadership. Instead, let's learn how to respond to it when it calls. So, did you answer the call to an executive title or to Leadership? I believe this is one of the most important questions we must answer before our Leadership presence can truly empower others to succeed.

People are the life force of any organization. The more you inspire them—the more you believe in and push them toward their Higher Self—the better they become. And when you pour into them, they will give you greater performance, productivity, and quality of work. This begins our journey to discovering the power to lead, engage, inspire, and transform those you lead and serve. This is the work of true Leadership. This power to lead only originates from the Spirit of Leadership. The Spirit of Leadership is the governing force that influences how you create meaningful, engaging connections with those you lead.

WHAT IS THE SPIRIT OF LEADERSHIP?

Before we define the Spirit of Leadership, let's take a moment to distinguish between a leader and a Leader. From the beginning of this chapter, I have been capitalizing Leader and Leadership. I believe there is a difference between *a leader* and *the Leader* and between *leadership* and *Leadership*. I will not make a long list of different traits and characteristics. Hopefully the following will suffice:

A leader is defined by the title and role someone gave her. She leads by the book and is careful not to push the envelope. She commits to maintaining status quo and pleasing those who enforce it.

The Leader is defined by the call to improve conditions to help others succeed. She knows the book and boldly decides to write new chapters (or a new book if necessary)! She commits to the call and the people who will be better because of it.

Which one are you?

As you lead, your energy will be invested in either:

1) Leading to not get fired.

2) Leading to maintain status quo, or

3) Leading to transform and disrupt things.

A leader is numbers one and two. The Leader is number three.

Again, which one are you?

The Leader is the one that people feel connected to the most. Whether it is in an email, a live talk, team meeting, one-on-one, or conference call, the Leader readily engages those he leads and serves. People want to join his team, work with him on special projects, and be led by him. People believe in the Leader because the Leader believes in them. He speaks their language. He speaks for them. He is their voice. He advocates for them. He is one of them.

> ## This is what makes their Leadership a gift: it's not for the Leader, it's for those she leads and serves.

On the other hand, a leader is so consumed with keeping his job that he doesn't make time to build true relationships with his team. Getting too personal with people makes him feel vulnerable, as if his authority is threatened. When he is vulnerable, he feels unable to protect himself which puts his position at risk. It's all about performance and pleasing the higher ups. He becomes consumed with making sure his team hits their numbers. He is fascinated with keeping the appearance of being busy. While he would benefit from spending time getting to know his team, he feels he needs to spend time protecting himself, watching his back, and wondering who on the team is a supporter or foe.

I could write a long list of differences between a leader and the Leader. The most important thing to note is that the Leader's ability to connect originates from the Spirit of Leadership. What pushes their performance is not company pay or benefits. While these perks are valuable, the Leader is inspired by something more. And this "something more" causes the Leader to take out their pen and write a more perfect future for those they lead and serve. This is what makes their Leadership a gift: it's not for the Leader, it's for those she leads and serves.

Here's my definition of the Spirit of Leadership:

It is the Convicting Power that moves us to say yes to the vision, work, and risk of making things remarkably better for others.

When the Spirit of Leadership is upon you, you begin to lead from a more connected part of yourself. It translates us from a local state of purpose to a global state of purpose. You begin to see more broadly. You connect with the mission, values, purpose, and people at a deeper level. The paycheck is great, but it doesn't drive you. What drives you is your yes. Many of the Leaders we admire are those who simply said yes to the vision, work, and risk of making things remarkably better for others.

The Spirit of Leadership is not the gift. It is, however, the essence and manner in which we present the gift called Leadership to others. The Spirit of Leadership represents how one searches for the perfect gift to give to a certain special someone. It asks the question, "Will this gift make their world better and make them better for their world?" It is not about the cost. The only thing that matters is that the recipient is worth the gift. Leadership is a gift worth an extremely high value. If Leadership is the gift, then the Spirit of Leadership is the true worth and value of the gift.

The Spirit of Leadership is the platform that exposes the Leader's purpose and intent. The Spirit of Leadership empowered Moses to declare to Pharaoh, "Let My People Go!" America's forefathers built the United States from this Spirit. The Declaration of Independence itself was a symbol of the vision, work, and risk of making things remarkably better for future citizens of America. In

1776 during the beginning of the American Revolution, Thomas Jefferson wrote:

> *"We hold these truths to be self-evident, that all men are created equal, that they are endowed by their Creator with certain unalienable Rights, that among these are Life, Liberty, and the pursuit of happiness."*

These very words were the foundation that shaped America, the Civil Rights Movement, and future movements that continue to create and sustain freedoms today.

Dr. Martin Luther King, Jr. was empowered by the Spirit of Leadership and addressed to the world "I have a dream," exposing the injustice of Black Americans in America. Mother Theresa served the poor from this Spirit. My friend, Terrance Stone, CEO of Young Visionaries in San Bernardino, CA coaches and mentors young men in juvenile hall from this same Spirit. He works tirelessly and selflessly to reduce recidivism for young men of color. Ronald J. Mittelstaedt, Founder, Chairman, and former CEO of the Fortune 500 conglomerate, Waste Connections, Inc. built the company's entire leadership development model on the Spirit of Leadership and being a servant Leader. From the Spirit of Leadership, we hear the words of Jesus echoing in eternity, "I didn't come to be served, but to serve" (Matthew 20:28).

One of my mentors, Dr. Judy White, served for more than forty years as an educator. In 2016 she was appointed the County Superintendent for Riverside County Office of Education. Under her leadership, teachers became principals, principals became school district executives, school district executives became superintendents, and students thrived at the highest levels and increased in academic success and graduation rates. Her entire life work was creating equitable pathways for others to succeed at the highest level. This was the only reason she accepted the opportunity to ascend to this top Leadership position. Though appointed, she never learned how to "politic." She just simply showed up every day leading from the Spirit of Leadership.

History reveals other greats who have been empowered by this Spirit. President Abraham Lincoln, who was not the brightest nor most experienced presidential candidate during his election, displayed the Spirit of Leadership and won the election of 1850. Through this Convicting Power, he was able to get opposing sides to come reason together. He also defied the odds and united the North and the Confederate South while opposing slavery. The late Nelson Mandela, as president of South Africa, embraced the Spirit of Leadership as he sought racial reconciliation in a country that once imprisoned him for twenty-seven years.

Bishop Charles Edward Blake, pastor emeritus of West Angeles Church of God in Christ in Los Angeles, California, built a powerful movement called, "Save Africa's Children," an initiative to fight against the HIV/AIDS pandemic in Africa. On any given Sunday you can find such famous people as Magic and Cookie Johnson or Denzel and Paulette Washington worshiping in the large 5,000-seat sanctuary. Yet, in his more than fifty years of pastoring, he never boasted about the famous people who attended West Angeles. He simply focused on using his influence to make things remarkably better for others.

My friend Josie Martin leads an organization called Dream Girls. Her global organization touches young girls from Los

Angeles to South Africa, teaching them about purity and self-confidence. She spends months with them and charges them nothing to be a part of the program. This is the Spirit of Leadership. Are you getting it? Is the Spirit of Leadership becoming more clear? Let's dig a little deeper.

> # The Spirit of Leadership manifests once the heart can no longer stand to see things remain the same.

Over and over again you see how Leaders said yes to the vision, work, and risk of making things remarkably better for others. Their fame is not necessarily in how much money they make or how popular they are. Their fame is in their yes. Here are just a few other indicators of The Spirit of Leadership:

- A teacher forsakes higher pay to teach in a lower income neighborhood.
- A college graduate enlists as an officer in the military to serve his or her country.
- A Fortune 500 CEO takes a pay cut so he doesn't have to lay off employees during a recession.
- Someone walks into the street and directs traffic to make sure a dog gets safely across.

- A member of a faith-based organization starts a food pantry for families in need.
- A volunteer dedicates his time to tutor kids after school to keep them from failing.
- A busy executive reschedules a meeting to take time to listen to an employee who is struggling.
- A theater director creates internships so she can pass on her directing skills to an interested youth.
- A doctor donates her time to respond to medical humanitarian emergencies in foreign countries.
- A lawyer takes on a pro bono case for someone unable to pay to ensure access to justice.

And the list could go on and on.

The Spirit of Leadership manifests once the heart can no longer stand to see things remain the same. Whether in the private, public, or social sector, the Spirit of Leadership begins the moment you put yourself on the hook and say, "This can't remain the same. I have to do something about it!" Regardless of the risk, you commit to doing something about it. The Spirit of Leadership won't allow you to remain quiet or passive. It drives you to do something.

This is Leadership. This is the gift we get to give away to others. It is not handed to us. We do not receive it as an award. It is an encounter with destiny. We saw something that needed to be changed and we were compelled to find solutions to change it. These are the Leaders who hear of a problem or an opportunity to change lives and simply say yes. They don't know why they said yes. They just know they had to say yes. Life would not be the same if they hadn't. They would literally feel they were cheating themselves if they didn't say yes. That compelling desire comes from the Spirit of Leadership. The Spirit of Leadership always precedes transformation.

Leadership can occur at any organizational level. It is not a title. It's not a position. It is considerate and sometimes disruptive. This kind of Leadership can make people on both sides (those who are for you and those who are against you) feel uneasy. Why? Because the Leader is not subject to the applause of the crowd but by the need for change. If they hear no, they find another way. For the Leader, asking for permission is an act of honor, not a necessity for moving forward. This is difficult because most leaders are taught to color within the lines. They would never dare to challenge the higher ups or status quo. And so, they become pawns. They don't rock the boat. They miss the chance to become the transformational Leader they are called to be. They don't get to make things remarkably better for others.

However, the Leader is not afraid to ask why. They are not disrespectful; they just aren't satisfied with doing it the old way when there is obviously a better way to make things better for others. This is the Leader that people want to follow and work with.

INTERNAL INDICATORS OF THE SPIRIT OF LEADERSHIP

How do you know when you are leading from the Spirit of Leadership? Here are four internal indicators I have noticed over the years:

1) You have a Global Vision.
2) You have an inexplicable faith and conviction to do something now.
3) You are willing to make the sacrifice.
4) You want to see others win.

YOU HAVE A GLOBAL VISION

One way to know that you are leading from the Spirit of Leadership is that your vision is much bigger than you. This vision is not self-centered nor self-promoting. It lifts everyone from the executive office to the frontline staff to the end user. When you have a global vision, you feel more inclined to take the organization past where it has gone before. Not because you want notoriety, but because it makes things remarkably better for others. You see the need to write a new chapter or book that opens new opportunities for the people you lead and serve.

Yvon Chouinard is an environmentalist, outdoorsman, climber, and the founder and former owner of Patagonia. Around the late 1960s, he saw a need for durable clothing that could withstand the severe conditions of rock and alpine climbing. So in 1973, he began making lasting outdoor wear and named the company Patagonia, headquartered in Ventura, California. From the beginning, Patagonia has focused on ethical and environmental issues and have embedded these issues in their core values. After barely surviving the economic downturn of the 1990s, Chouinard refocused his mission and core values to align with a global vision: protecting the environment, social causes, community, and sustainability. He held a strong conviction that civilization would cease to exist if human beings didn't take better care of the planet they inhabited.

In 2022, Chouinard announced that he was giving up ownership in Patagonia to the Patagonia Purpose Trust to protect the company's values and ensure profits would be used for addressing climate change. He wrote on Patagonia's website, "Instead of 'going public,' you could say we're 'going purpose.'"[1] Regardless of one's opinion of Chouinard's actions, no one can mistake his commitment to saying yes to the vision, work, and risk of making things remarkably better for others.

As the Leader, you must establish a purpose and vision that extends beyond you. In my opinion, every business, corporation, religious institution, school, and invention should have a global vision that empowers people to succeed. Some may call it a B-Corp, others may call it Corporate Social Responsibility. I call it a Purposeful Organization. Patagonia became a billion-dollar company. If you are called to build a million or billion dollar company, then I pray you succeed. I also pray, as Chouinard did with Patagonia, that you are convicted by a global vision that drives you to build a great company with great products or services that make life better for others.

YOU HAVE AN INEXPLICABLE FAITH AND CONVICTION TO DO SOMETHING NOW

This second internal indicator means you feel compelled to lead. If change is going to happen, you have to step up and say yes now! The Convicting Power calls for you to throw your entire self

---

1 Yvon Chouinard, "Patagonia 50," Patagonia, Patagonia, Inc., 2023. https://www.patagonia.com/ownership/.

at a project or opportunity. You might be afraid and uncertain. You may not even know why you are drawn to such a cause or opportunity. But you still move forward. You believe your labor will not be in vain. You know that you will miss a valuable opportunity if you fail to say yes to it. As John Wanamaker once stated, "A man is not doing much until the cause he works for possesses all there is of him."

When I think about this inexplicable faith and conviction, I think of author and speaker Christine Caine. In 2007, Christine traveled from Australia to Greece to speak at a women's Christian conference. When she arrived at the airport in Thessaloniki, she learned that her luggage had somehow been delayed. While awaiting her luggage, she saw posters of missing young women. A bit curious, she went from poster to poster studying their faces. The faces of the young women lingered in her mind and the word *missing* wrenched her heart.

As difficult as it was to look at these pictures, Christine began wondering what had happened to these women. She soon learned that these young women were likely victims of human trafficking. At that time Christine knew very little about human trafficking. While it grabbed her attention, she didn't know how she could be of any help to these young ladies. She had already achieved great success as a speaker. Yet, the faces of these women and their plight kept her awake at night. She was convinced that she was being called to do something for them. This is when the inexplicable faith and conviction kicked in.

True Leaders know instinctively when it is time to step up and do something. An opportunity to change the course for others presents itself. The opportunity often shows up without notice. BAM! It appears before the Leader almost demanding an acceptance to its invitation. And for some reason, the Leader says yes. They say yes without knowing all the details. Despite the work and risk, they commit their lives right there in that moment to doing something to change the outcome of others. They don't say yes because they have the knowledge and expertise, they say yes because they are called to do it. Christine told herself that she didn't know enough about the issue. She didn't feel that she wasn't educated or skilled enough. Even more so, she felt the task was just too dangerous. And yet the Convicting Power moved her to say yes. Christine was being called to do something for these young ladies. And she said yes.

Christine and her husband Nick took a leap of faith. They believed that they were being called to rescue, restore, and rebuild the lives of human trafficking victims. They called their organization the A21 Campaign. A21 stands for "abolish injustice in the 21st century."[2] What they were attempting to do seemed insurmountable. They hired consultants to advise them on opening a safehouse in Thessaloniki, Greece. The consultants did not have the same conviction that Christine and Nick had. The consultants told them that there were too many factors working against them. They couldn't see any way that the A21 Campaign could be successful. Still, the Caines were certain of their vision and the necessary pieces began falling into place. Because they committed to their yes, their faith, and their conviction, they received financial backing, then moved to open their safehouse. They were told it

---

2   Christine Caine, "Christine Caine – The A21 Campaign" (blog), *End Slavery Now*, 2023. https://www.endslaverynow.org/blog/articles/christine-caine-the-a21-campaign.

would take at least two years to receive all the approvals and permits to open. Their lawyer turned in their application and made an impassioned plea for the cause of human trafficking victims. The same day, they received the necessary permit. There are now A21 offices throughout the world. The organization works to raise awareness of human trafficking, establish prevention programs, represent victims as legal advocates, and give these victims refuge in safe houses, then restoration in transition homes.

There is nothing more powerful than a faith-filled, convicted Leader that says yes to the opportunities to step up and change things for the better. You can be this Leader. You can get your team to rally around a global vision and infuse a faith culture into every department. Many of the executives I coach struggle leading with faith and conviction. They are too concerned with what others will say if they lead their organizations in a certain direction. They often succumb to groupthink. They say no when they should say yes. They say yes when they should say no. But the Leader reviews the information, considers the data and research, listens to the experts, and then makes a decision. The Leader knows opportunities do not hang around long. As Leonard Ravenhill once said, "The opportunity of a lifetime must be seized in the lifetime of the opportunity." Leaders stay ready and move in faith.

YOU ARE WILLING TO MAKE THE SACRIFICE

The third internal indicator of leading from the Spirit of Leadership is that you are not afraid to put on the gloves and do the hard work. Your team wants to know that you will go the extra mile. They should be convinced that you are right there with them in the fight. The people you lead and serve should see that you have placed a lot on the line and that you are fully vested in the vision. Loyalty increases when people know that the Leader is all in.

When it comes to a Leader who has made great sacrifices, my friend Sam Itani comes to mind. Sam is the CEO of Corona Regional Medical Center (CRMC) in Corona, CA, and a former client of mine. Before becoming CEO of CRMC, Sam served as the COO of a hospital in Bakersfield, CA, about 156 miles northwest of Corona. While leading in Bakersfield, Sam had the desire to one day become the CEO of a hospital. He wanted to be a CEO to bring about greater transformational change for both hospital staff and patients. Sam knew that if he could get to a CEO position, he could really achieve something great. He had many ideas, but they were difficult to implement because he was not the CEO. A recruiter soon called him about a COO position that opened up at a hospital in Palmdale, CA. He was told this position would eventually lead him to a CEO role. However, the recruiter thought Sam would be a better fit as the CEO of a hospital in Corona. The CEO of the hospital in Corona was retiring and Sam would come in as COO for a few months and then take over as CEO after the current CEO retired. They eventually offered him the position of COO in Palmdale and said he could have it if he wanted it. But Sam said he felt God leading him to Corona and that this was the place where he could bring about the greatest change.

CRMC made an offer to Sam, but it required some sacrifices on Sam's part. First, Sam took a huge pay cut to be the CEO of CRMC.

This means Sam's salary as COO would be less than his salary as CEO. Second, he would obviously have to move from Bakersfield to Corona. Thirdly, His wife Ghina had a business in Bakersfield and had grown it to where she now had many clients. He said he believed God had a plan for him in Corona but he would have to make a sacrifice. Sam got his family together and listed the pros and cons. Sam told me that the cons outweighed the pros. But they still felt they needed to make the move. This was the beginning of Sam saying yes to the vision, work, and risk of making things remarkably better for others.

Keep in mind that they knew no one in Corona. All they had was their faith to believe that this sacrifice was necessary. In March 2021, Sam began his career in Corona as COO and then a few months later became CEO.

Sam knew this CEO role was not going to be a glamorous role in the beginning. At the time, CRMC did not have the greatest reputation in Corona among residents. Many residents would drive more than forty miles past CRMC to go to another hospital. On top of this, Sam began as CEO during the height of the COVID-19 pandemic, when restaurants, malls, and almost all public facilities were closed. How could Sam build the hospital's reputation when he would not be able to connect with the community? How would he be able to lead the hospital to the next level when nurses and doctors were quitting while patient count rose, revenue was down, and they were running out of beds and space for sick patients and protective gear for staff?

Sam knew he would have to make major sacrifices just to help CRMC survive the pandemic, let alone rebuild its image within the city of Corona. Nevertheless, Sam rolled up his sleeves and went to work. He brought his executive team together and cast a vision. Not just a vision of survival, but a vision to make CRMC the destination of choice for healthcare. He let them know of the sacrifices that each would need to make to get through the COVID-19 pandemic. He did not just spell out his executive team's sacrifice, but he also shared his own. Whether it was working in the supply and delivery department to make sure doctors and nurses had their supplies, helping the custodial staff clean bathrooms and mop floors, or even working in the cafeteria to help the dietitians prepare breakfast, lunch, and dinner for patients and staff. Sam was willing to do whatever was necessary to keep CRMC afloat and moving forward.

Many leaders would have walked into this situation and immediately felt they made the biggest mistake of their life. Some leaders would have remained in their C-suite office and left the menial tasks to the frontline staff. As if they were too good to get down and dirty. But as I mentioned before, the Leader knows that her teams need to see that she's placed a lot on the line. She understands that this builds loyalty and will ultimately increase her team's sacrifice, performance, and productivity.

As the city of Corona began to open its public spaces, Sam immediately went out into the city to get connected. If there was a community event, Sam was there. When nonprofit organizations had events, Sam was there. Many wondered why Sam was spending so much time connecting with the community. They had not seen previous CEOs do this before. Other leaders before him were tied to the office. But Sam understood the assignment and the assignment called for sacrifice. If CRMC was going to be the destination of choice, there would be sacrifice and Sam would be the Chief Sacrificial Officer. Sam once told me that the success of any organization was a byproduct of the sacrifice the Leader makes.

As the Leader, you must be willing to be uncomfortable. Too many leaders want to live up to the glamor of their title and position. This separates you from the people you need to show up and do the work much more than it connects you to them. The gift you give to your team is sacrifice. You are modeling to your team what it takes to make things happen. And at the end of the sacrifice, you celebrate. Sam would often place high-impact projects before his team, give a deadline, and when they succeeded, he celebrated their win—big.

YOU WANT TO SEE OTHERS WIN

As the Leader, you should never be intimated by anyone's desire to excel. At the end of the day, you should want people to live, work, collaborate, and experience the world better than before. Leaders are comfortable in their own skin. They are not envious when the people they lead succeed. They never try to hold people back from achieving their dreams and goals. In fact, they understand that helping others prepare for greater success is a part of their Leadership role. The Leader realizes what matters is not how high he rises, but how high he helps others rise through his Leadership.

There are a few Leaders I could write about whom I believe were excellent at positioning others for greater success. There are not many, but their stories would serve as awesome examples of what it looks like for the Leader to help others win. But I would rather tell a story about you. The near future you, that is. The you that is becoming an even more effective you as a result of reading this book.

You are the Leader, and you lead a successful organization. Your organization is not successful because of its profits. Your organization is successful because of its people. You built your organization on the principle that the people who work there are the most important asset. Leadership to you means making sure your team is equipped and empowered to deliver quality results. You create a high-performance culture where people are measured not just by how much they produce, but who they become. As a result, other Leaders in your organization are often found mentoring up-and-coming Leaders. Job performance is not just based on hitting numbers or other metrics. Performance is learning, trying, failing, learning some more, collaborating, being a team player, making the sacrifice, and growing and getting better after. When you treat them well, they will ultimately treat your clients well.

You do your best to put people in positions that reflect their natural gifts and passion. You do not set them up to fail by placing them in positions where you know they will not thrive. This not only negatively impacts the person, but it impedes productivity for your organization. You would rather slow down and get them placed in the most effective roles that enhance their capacity, as well as the organization's. This is one stage of wanting to see others win. But there is another stage that is more difficult.

Although you pour yourself into helping others win, it is more joyful when their winning means promoting within your organization. However, as the Leader, you realize that helping others win also means helping them prepare for Leadership roles outside of your organization. A leader would frown upon this. It makes absolutely no sense to them to spend that much time pouring into someone who might eventually leave and possibly go to a competitor. Why would a leader do that? Well, they wouldn't. Only the Leader would. You are the Leader who understands that whether they stay or go to another organization, you planted the seed. This is an attraction to others who are looking to get promoted into Leadership one day. They know that if they can work with you, they have the potential to be promoted and eventually lead within the organization or within another. And now you are not only known for the products you sell or the services you offer, but you are also known for empowering human beings to achieve their highest potential both personally and professionally.

My attempt here is to help you see your Future Self so clearly as if you were looking into a mirror. I want you to see yourself as the Leader that people love to follow and work with. You will be at your best as you help others to be at their best. Your team members give all to your organization because you give all to them. Performance evaluations are an opportunity for you to help your team get stronger. You do not look to find the flaws or what they did wrong. You look for opportunities for them to grow. Here's what you know: when they win, everyone wins! Let this future Leader that you are becoming be your guiding force. This is the Leader who makes things remarkably better for others.

EXTERNAL INDICATORS OF THE SPIRIT OF LEADERSHIP

Leadership is the fruit from the seeds (internal indicators) one plants over time. While these internal indicators are developing underground, there are also outward expressions of these internal indicators that can be observed and measured. External indicators include:

1) You serve others well.
2) You commit to personal growth and growing others.
3) You design equitable systems, frameworks, and pathways that simplify and improve the quality and impact of the work.

Let's dig deeper into these three external indicators.

SERVING

Leadership tends to be inherent among those who are willing to serve first. Many do not like the term Servant Leadership. However, serving does not mean weak or soft. It doesn't even mean less than or of a lower class. My definition of serving is being well-trained, equipped, skilled, intelligent, knowledgeable, of the highest quality, attentive, and precise with the sole intent of making life and work remarkably better for others.

Whether someone is serving you food at a restaurant, washing your car, driving you around town, dry cleaning your clothes, fixing your A/C unit, managing your investments, giving you a manicure, or whatever else, you want to be served well. You have never hired anyone to do a quality job, received subpar service, and said, "Oh, well, they're just serving. I'll pay them, but I don't expect them to do a good job." You place a high demand on how they deliver a product or service to you and will demand a refund if they don't. Why? Because you expect them to provide top-quality service.

You even pay a premium for "option three" because you believe the service will be of even greater quality than options one and two, and include a better protection guarantee or warranty. There is a certain level of excellence that is demanded by serving. And the same goes for you as the Leader. However, no matter how good the food is at the restaurant or no matter how comfortable the bed feels at the resort, if you do not receive top customer service, you probably will not utilize that brand again. You might even write a one-star review to alert others not to use their service.

Serving people well attracts loyalty. Think about it. The restaurant you frequent for lunch. The hotel chain or resort you prefer or even your choice airline. We tend to choose these companies because of their quality of service. We like how we feel when we stay at a certain resort or drive a certain car. They pay attention to us and make us feel better than we really are. In return for this service, we pay more money because the service is worth it. We tell others about our experience and invite them to use the same brand.

The key to serving is paying attention. It is noticing what people need, often before they even know they need it or ask. The Spirit of Leadership calls for you to pay attention. You look for ways to make people better and improve systems to allow them to be more effective. You notice blockage to performance, productivity, and quality of work and do what you can to remove it.

This is you as the Leader. People love to follow and work with you because you give the gift of serving. You pay attention to them. You are precise. People feel they matter to you. And so, they show up better, whole, and ready to collaborate and get things done.

It has been said that, "Organizations are established to serve human needs. There is no other reason for their existence." James Cash Penney (J.C. Penney) once said, "A merchant who approaches business with the idea of serving the public well has nothing to fear from the competition."[3]

GROWING

If serving means well-trained, equipped, skilled, intelligent, knowledgeable, high quality, attentive, and precise with the sole intent of making life and work better for others, then growing is how we become better at serving others. Your organization will not outgrow you. If the organization does not have a growing Leader, then the organization will not grow. I often say, "Whether your organization is healthy, dysfunctional, or stuck . . . it ALWAYS acts like its leader!" Your organization is the size of you. It is the size of your training. It is as equipped as you are. It is no more skilled than you are. CEOs are often fired because they fail to grow. As the Leader, one of your number one jobs is personal and professional development. As you grow, so grows the organization. This does however depend on whether you are leading in the right place.

3   James Cash Penney–a merchant who approaches business...–brainyquote, n.d., https://www.brainyquote.com/quotes/james_cash_penney_226519.

Almost every book I've ever read about great organizations mentions the quality of time the Leader spent investing inn his personal and professional development. Your vision requires a different kind of Leader than you are right now. Let's face it. You are not smart enough, skilled enough, or knowledgeable enough to lead at the level of your vision. Therefore, growth is required. Leadership growth should not be an afterthought. It must be intentional and purposeful. As a matter of fact, pause from reading this book and have your executive assistant (or whoever handles your calendar) schedule forty-five minutes every day for personal development.

I can truthfully tell you that my income has always grown when I took the time to invest in my personal and professional development. The caliber of my clients grew as I grew. As I developed professionally, CEOs began to trust that I was able to coach them and their executive team as opposed to only working with their managers and supervisors.

But allow me to digress for a moment. I believe organizational Leaders should also be great Leaders at home. A piece of you will always be missing if you have not learned to lead well within your family. You cannot be as sharp and focused on your organization when you are not well connected with your family at home. I am not saying you cannot lead a great organization without being a great leader at home. I am saying you are not a complete Leader and will never feel right leading in your organization if you are failing to be a Leader in your home. Why is this important? Because the first institution ever established was the family. Before businesses, corporations, institutions, or any organization, there was the family.

The Leader not only displays this external indicator of growing, but also encourages others to grow in an applicable manner. She realizes that when she makes others better, she will get better. And this is the only measurement of success to her. Who are you making better?

Personal and professional growth does not happen in a vacuum. It is intentional. It is not just attending a conference, hiring a coach, or reading a book. Growth is contingent upon the vision. Who is the vision requiring you and your team to be? How do you need to shift your mindset, beliefs, language, and behaviors to make things better for others?

DESIGNING

If you are leading from the Spirit of Leadership, then you figure out ways to design systems and frameworks that simplify and improve the quality and impact of the work produced by your team. The Leader thinks in terms of how to make things simpler for people to work, work together, and get things done. This is a reason the Leader challenges the status quo. They do not want to disrupt just to disrupt. But if they see there is a better way, they don't see why it shouldn't be enacted and implemented.

Designing is one of the key skills of the Leader. This does not mean they have the gift of designing. It simply means they spend time looking. The Leader focuses on the whole system and asks, "How can we make this better?" or, "How can we be more efficient?" They then gather a team of analysts with specialized skills to help create pathways to produce better products faster without losing quality or provide greater service for their clients.

The Leader understands it takes a lot of work to achieve the vision. Anyone else would say it is too hard. But the Leader designs. This means she cannot accept that there is not a way to make it happen. Maybe it will take more time. Maybe there is more knowledge to ascertain. Or maybe the right talent just needs to be hired. Whatever the case, the Leader is going to go into design mode. Designing for the Leader is answering the who, what, when, and how of the strategy. Designing is building the bridge from here to there. Since the vision comes from the Leader, the Leader should be responsible for gathering the team to design opportunities to move toward the vision.

The Leader spends massive amounts of time looking at the whole and how each part works with the others.

BECOMING THE LEADER

Is a Leader born or made? Honestly? It really doesn't matter! That is not important. What is important is that you are responding to the Spirit of Leadership. The Spirit of Leadership first shows up as a defining moment. Something in your organization, your industry, or world is thrown off course from its original purpose and therefore Leadership is necessary. Again, the Leader doesn't need a title; she just needs a reason. She isn't satisfied just sitting by allowing things to remain the same. If no one speaks, she will speak up. If no one moves, she will say yes to the vision, work, and risk of making things remarkably better for others.

Leadership does not appear when someone is asked to fill a leadership position. It does not happen when someone gets an executive title added to their name. Nor does it happen when a candidate is voted into office. Leadership happens long before. It happens when those internal indicators I mentioned above begin to erupt within their spirit. These internal indicators cause a person to come to work early and stay late to make sure their team stays ahead on their project. Leadership appears when people take time from their job to help someone figure something out. Leadership is a lifestyle, not a position.

Leadership shows up as a defining moment. Like in the movie *The Matrix*, you are presented with two future options (the blue or red pill): One option (the blue pill) says, "*You'll live a normal, mediocre life, work hard, stay below the radar, and people will soon forget any contribution you made after you leave.*"

The other option (the red pill) says, "*Your life will never be the same again. You'll put everything you have and love at risk. And it will be really scary. But nothing will be as satisfying, rewarding, and fulfilling as this. You will leave a legacy and you will impact many people.*" You were never planning to lead in this manner, but you're ready to say yes when it confronts you. You are ready because you were already doing the work.

People don't follow you; they follow the Spirit of Leadership on your life. They are following who they believe they can become and what they can be a part of by following your vision. This is what John C. Maxwell refers to as Level 5 Leadership. You represent a greater purpose. You stand for something that is bigger than the organization itself. You become an ambassador for human achievement. John Maxwell says, "People follow them because of who they are and what they represent. In other words, their leadership gains a positive reputation. As a result, Level 5 leaders often transcend their position, their organization, and sometimes their industry."[4]

The Spirit of Leadership shows up the moment someone serves a bigger purpose, without need of title, compensation, or recognition. This Leader doesn't seek a title. They are not waiting to be called on. They have learned to respond to necessity. They just say yes.

Leaders are not Leaders because they have a Leadership position. Leaders are Leaders because, at every level and in every position, they said yes to the vision, work, and risk of making things remarkably better for others.

Man cannot make you the Leader nor can he take it away from you. Necessity and opportunity call us to lead. An unwritten history confers Leadership upon us. True Leaders are inserted in certain moments of time to disrupt the status quo, not to maintain it. They can't be given a title by man. It was Divinely placed on them. Society is forced to make room for them. These Leaders are rising. Unconventional they are, but necessary.

Ego-driven leadership and organizations have met their fatal end. No one wants to work for such a leader or organization (unless they too are flawed and egocentric, but they will go down with the organization and its leadership). We are now living in an era where people want to be a part of something bigger than themselves. They want to find purpose, fulfillment, and joy in

---

4 John C. Maxwell, *The 5 Levels of Leadership: Proven Steps to Maximize Your Potential* (New York: Center Street, 2013).

everything they do. Anything that is seen less than this will experience dysfunction and opposition.

THE BOTTOM LINE IS PEOPLE

Leadership was not created for any specific industry. It was created for people. A leader can exist without money, an executive office, technology, bonuses and raises, promotions, a housing or car allowance, or fame. However, a leader cannot exist without people. You have never heard of any successful movement or corporate change initiative that did not include people.

If you desire to drive greater outcomes in your organization, you do it through transforming people. The Spirit of Leadership changes how you see success. It doesn't mean you stop focusing on growth. It doesn't mean profit is not important. The Leader knows the areas that are imperative to organizational success. But the Leader also understands the Spirit of Leadership changes how people work, how people work together, and the manner in which they get things done. Instead of you seeing tasks and assignments, you see how to get the right people on the bus and in the right seats and then determine which way is the best way to go.[5]

We can recall in history, from the nation of Israel in Old Testament times to the founding of America, to the freeing of black slaves in America in 1863, to the abolishing of apartheid in South Africa in 1994, how a Leader was used to accomplish national and global reformation. Whenever God wanted a nation transformed, He called for a Leader. He would raise up someone from the trenches or from an unlikely place and have them be light in

---

5 Jim Collins, *Good to Great: Why Some Companies Make the Leap and Others Don't* (Harper Business, 2001).

a dark world. If there were a people group who needed to be lifted from despair, He raised up a Leader. When a nation needed direction, a Leader was called forth. When an oppressed city or nation needed to be freed, a leader was called forth to utilize her skills to bring down injustice, raise hope, and liberate the people. Leaders are called to guard and prosper cities and nations in accordance with a Divine plan. Do you know the reason you have been called to lead your organization, city, or nation?

My point is not to preach to you, but to show you how leaders from all different backgrounds, eras, and professions led with the Spirit of Leadership. When there was darkness in their nation, they rose up and became light. They were a gift to others. The bottom line is this: nations, cities, schools, communities, corporations, and organizations succeed when Leaders are in authority.

The late Dr. Myles Munroe was known to often say, "Where purpose is not known, abuse is inevitable."[6] When we do not truly know, honor, and respect the Spirit of Leadership, we will not lead our organizations to its full potential. So this book is an invitation. It is saying, *Répondez s'il vous plait*, or RSVP. By beginning this book, you have taken the first step to responding. It is of great hope that you will continue up the steps to the Spirit of Leadership. It is a request for you to join the many local and global influencers who have stood on it before you and even those standing on it now and those who will mount it in the future. My hope is to empower you to know the Spirit of Leadership, honor and revere the Spirit of Leadership, live your life from the Spirit

---

of Leadership, and even, dare I say, die having given all from the Spirit of Leadership.

The rest of this book will show you how to engage and empower those you are leading and serving and become the Leader that people love to follow and work with.

Everything you will read from here on can only be released by the Spirit of Leadership. The following chapters are not individual gifts. They each encompass how the Gift called Leadership is offered to others. As in buying a gift for someone you care about, it isn't the gift itself that matters. It is the way you took time to know who they are, their desires, wants, and needs, and the environment and manner in which the gift was given to them. You are the gift that people need. It is your Leadership presence that empowers others to succeed. Let's prepare you to give your best so you can get the best out of the people you lead and serve. The rest of this book will provide you a detailed explanation of the kind of language and behaviors that inspire people to follow and work with you.

—— CHAPTER 2 ——

BE SELF-AWARE AND FULLY PRESENT

B*eing self-aware and fully present, in my opinion, is the foun-*dation to becoming the Leader that empowers others to succeed. It is what makes the Gift called Leadership most receptive to others. A leader can never commit to becoming the gift that people need until he recognizes whether he has the ability to impact how people live, work, collaborate, and see the world. This is crucial to anyone who desires to be the Leader. Staying in tune with who you are being and your impact on others is highly important. I often encourage Leaders to not only focus on organizational goals but personal and Leadership development goals as well. As I mentioned earlier, "Whether your organization is healthy, dysfunctional, or stuck . . . it ALWAYS acts like its leader!"

Being self-aware and fully present is the Leader's superpower. It's being cognizant of how you show up in a person's world. This means knowing how your leadership is being presented and accepted among those you lead and serve. People need to know you get them, that you understand how their world operates and how they view the world. As the Leader, you cannot allow your mental models to cause you to dismiss another's view of life.

BE SELF-AWARE

Self-awareness is a part of the gift we give to those we lead and serve. Self-awareness is a process of learning and growing. As things change at a rapid pace, it forces us to have to learn, adjust, and adapt to these changes as quickly as possible. Our survival depends on it. So, self-awareness is not a destination. It is a journey. People will give their best to you as you commit yourself to the journey.

If the Spirit of Leadership is the true north of Leadership, then self-awareness is:

The ability to recognize opportunities to learn, grow, and operate more fully from the Spirit of Leadership.

When we break down the definition, we see that the Leader must do three things:

1) Recognize opportunities to learn.
2) Recognize opportunities to grow.
3) Recognize opportunities to operate more fully from the Spirit of Leadership.

RECOGNIZE OPPORTUNITIES TO LEARN

The Leader never stops learning. Your team should also take note of this. The Leader is constantly listening inward and outward. She is in tune with her self-talk and determines the source behind her intentions. The Leader who is self-aware is not afraid of 360-degree assessments. She welcomes input (good, bad, or ugly) from her team. She listens objectively to their comments. It sometimes stings and hurts, but she listens to learn. As she learns, she gets to know her team, their fears, uncertainties, hopes, and aspirations. She realizes it is her job to grow others and grow herself at the same time. Self-awareness is recognizing opportunities to learn how to listen to your Higher Self as well as to others.

It is extremely challenging to be around someone who is unwilling to learn. A leader who refuses to learn forfeits the opportunity to realize how their Leadership can cause others to be and give their best. In 2014, I was tasked with coaching a mid-level manager in a large organization in San Francisco. Let's call her Sabrina. Sabrina's director called me and told me about the complaints she was getting about Sabrina. The team found Sabrina to be cold, not concerned about anyone's feelings as she "told them what to do." She lacked empathy. If Sabrina didn't like you, you knew it. I agreed to coach Sabrina only if she was willing to be coached. I felt this would be a good challenge for me. I had no idea what I was getting myself into.

Sabrina set a clear outcome for our coaching. She even liked the idea of ridding her team of the dysfunction they were experiencing since the day she became the manager. Our sessions began well. We communicated very well with each other. However, I could tell something was off. Sabrina and I were scheduled for two sessions per month for six months. Twelve sessions total. But we didn't make it past eight. Sabrina was not able to recognize opportunities to listen and learn. would she even consider someone else's side. Anytime we talked about the issues on the team and her 360 evaluations, Sabrina would immediately begin telling me about how sorry her team was (she even said this out loud to them in a team session we had). In her eyes, it was them and not her. One of the challenges I find when coaching executives is to get them to objectively listen to what others are saying without becoming defensive. Too often leaders hear critical feedback and feel it is an attack on their character. They feel blamed and shamed. One question I often ask when two or more parties are involved in a conflict is, "What is your contribution to the problem you are trying to solve?" I have found this to be a great way for even the most innocent to explore how they can learn and grow in a challenging situation. Sabrina committed to not playing any role in her team's conflict. She never listened to her team. To her, everything was an attack. Long story short, I called the director after our eighth session and told her she probably would want to move Sabrina to a different department. Specifically, a non-leadership role. The director took my advice and now that team is thriving without Sabrina.

RECOGNIZE OPPORTUNITIES TO GROW

Leaders learn, then they grow. I mentioned earlier that one of the external indicators of the Spirit of Leadership is that the Leader commits to personal growth. Personal growth can come from hiring a coach or asking someone to be a mentor or advisor to help them break through limiting beliefs and behaviors. Their growth is not dictated by themselves alone. They depend on and value the input from their mentors and coaches and the people they lead to determine whether growth has truly taken place. Leaders want both quantitative and qualitative feedback. The former tells them how much they have grown. The latter tells them the impact of their growth.

One of our clients is a great example of a leader who wanted to learn and grow. Rasheed Terry and his wife Michelle are owners of Point Target Fitness, a health club located in Redondo Beach, CA. Rasheed had heard me speak at an event he attended and later asked if I'd be his coach. He realized his business would only be as successful as his ability to grow as a leader. Very admittingly, Rasheed expressed how his lack of confidence was getting in the way of growing his business. The great thing about Rasheed is his willingness to tell the truth and be open and honest with himself and others, especially his wife.

Rasheed was not only open to learning but also open to growing. He realized he was the ceiling to his company's growth. The limits on his Leadership were the limits on his vision and team. As I mentioned before, your organization acts just like you. If you lack confidence, your organization will lack confidence. If you are indecisive, your organization will act indecisive. If your leadership limit is a five but your vision requires you to be a seven, then your team and organization will never grow past a five. They will not outgrow your growth. This is what John Maxwell refers to as the Law of the Lid[7]. The only way your organization will grow is when you grow. You want a better team? You want a better organization? Grow and become a better leader. This is self-awareness. This is growth. Personal growth is your gift to those you lead and serve.

---

7   John C. Maxwell, *The 21 Irrefutable Laws of Leadership: Follow Them and People Will Follow You* (New York, NY: HarperCollins Leadership, 2007).

After our fourth session, Rasheed had such a powerful breakthrough that he emailed me to share his growth:

Good morning Coach,

I felt led to share with you how impactful our last coaching session was. I'm very thankful that you tell it like it is, you ask the hard questions, and you are not afraid to tell me "Let it GO" [limitations I placed on myself]. I appreciate that because it puts me in a mindset to really get things going in our business. It was refreshing and gave me clarity. I feel overwhelmed with gratitude this morning and just wanted to share this with you. I can't wait to see where God takes us in the next thirty days. You have definitely added value to our lives.

Blessings,

Rasheed Terry

The simple steps Rasheed took to grow are the same steps any Leader must take to grow. These steps include:

1) *A goal for growth:* With the help of your coach, set a specific, measurable, and actionable growth goal.

2) *A commitment to growth:* In order to give your best, you must commit to increasing your capacity to lead.

3) *A coach/mentor for growth:* All great athletes, leaders, and influencers have coaches. Hiring a coach shows you have committed to growth.

4) *A pathway for growth:* Come up with three to five steps that will lead you to your growth goal.

5) *Indicators of growth:* Define what growth looks like at each step along the pathway. Growth is deliberate. Measure it.

6) *Accountability for growth:* Allow the people you lead and serve to watch you grow, support you as you grow, and be a part of your growth.

7) *Celebration of growth:* Celebrations are for achieving goals. Make sure you do it well. But don't celebrate you. Celebrate how others will increase because of your growth. Remember, your growth is a gift for them.

Recognizing opportunities to grow is not about knowing how to get it right, it's about knowing when to get better.

RECOGNIZE OPPORTUNITIES TO OPERATE MORE FULLY FROM THE SPIRIT OF LEADERSHIP

Think about the many demands on your Leadership. How many meetings do you attend in a week? How many deadlines do you have to meet? How many one-on-ones do you have? You can easily become overwhelmed just by thinking of the constant pull on your time in your Leadership role. But these are prime opportunities to "practice" operating more fully from the Spirit of Leadership. Each of these encounters include people who depend on you to lead them. Whether I am in a meeting, a one-on-one coaching session, or speaking from stage, I do my best to be self-aware of the following:

- It's not about me.
- I don't know it all. So be humble, listen, and learn.
- Operate from the state of love, hope and faith, and peace.
- Serve them well and make things remarkably better for them.

Being self-aware of these areas helps me to operate more fully from the Spirit of Leadership. However, I must admit there were times in my Leadership journey where I did the exact opposite of what I just wrote above. There is no way I can write such a book without being honest and transparent about my own leadership disappointments. In a previous organization I led, I had great people leave simply because every time I spoke, I made it about me. One team member even asked me, "Do you realize how much you talk about yourself in meetings?" Ouch! At the time I did not realize how insecure I was. My leadership was not a gift for them. I did not make things remarkably better for others. Instead, I thought that promoting myself made me look better or smarter in their eyes.

But thankfully I soon learned that Leadership is for the people I lead and serve. "I" soon became "you," "we," and "us." People began to feel they were a priority whenever they were in my presence. I noticed that when I made my team top priority, showed up with a humble spirit, operated from the state of love, hope and faith, and peace, and when I served them well, their performance, productivity, and quality of work increased. Operating more fully from the Spirit of Leadership increased my capacity to get the best out of them.

Operating more fully from the Spirit of Leadership is a higher realm than the personal growth mentioned previously. This is purposeful growth. What's the difference? Personal growth is internal. It is only measured by the increase within you. Purposeful growth is external. It is measured by the impact of how your personal growth causes others to increase and positions them, both individually and collectively, to drive greater impact and change. Purposeful growth is when you expand your capacity to serve others well. It is when you provide professional development opportunities to equip and empower them to increase their performance, productivity, and quality of work. Purposeful growth also includes designing equitable pathways for people to thrive and succeed. These are the external indicators I mentioned in the previous chapter. This is the gift people need from their leaders. They want to look into your vision and see themselves thriving even more. So, take time to create an inspiring vision. They want to follow your Leadership knowing that you're standing with them in the good and challenging times. So, connect with people. They want to know that whatever decision you make, even though they may not agree, they believe you considered them and their input. So, honor and respect people. This is how you get the best out of the people you lead and serve.

I was once asked to work with an executive leadership team from a mission-driven legal firm. My job for the two-day retreat was to help them recreate their vision statement, begin the work to design their strategic plan, and get back to their mission. The executive director and board president admitted that things had become a bit disjointed over the years. Not to mention, during that time they were all dealing with the COVID-19 pandemic that shut many businesses down. This also prohibited them from gathering in person as a team. Through some assessments, we quickly discovered that COVID-19 simply amplified the issues that were already prevalent prior to the pandemic. Strangely, they had written their most recent draft of their vision nineteen years before. Unfortunately, no one even knew where to find a copy of the vision. The majority of the new board members and executive team didn't even know what the vision was. The organization and its leaders had moved so far away from purposeful growth that they struggled to find meaning to the work they did. So over the years, they kept losing members on the board and some great quality staff members. The new board president and executive director wanted to put an end to this.

We spent the first two and a half hours working through our framework for drafting a vision. I wanted to make sure we connected everyone back to the reason they existed. So, I had them discuss the following:

- What matters most to you about the work (mission) of your organization (philosophically)?
- Why does this matter to your clients (philosophically)

After we split them into groups to discuss this, we saw that many of them looked past their differences and conflicts and connected on common themes. After the close of the day, growth was not about how many clients they needed to see or did they do this or that. Growth became much more purposeful for them. They wanted to know about their impact, not just their numbers. Those metrics became more important to them.

Here are a few indicators that purposeful growth is taking place (or you are operating more fully from the Spirit of Leadership) in your organization:

1) The team feels connected with the Leader.

2) People take ownership of their work.

3) The performance, productivity, and quality of work increases.

4) Sick leave/stress leave reduces.

5) Retention increases.

6) People grow in empathy.

7) People ask, "How are you doing?" and genuinely care about the answer.

8) The team supports each other when the workload is heavy.

9) The Leader hears concerns and does something about it.

10) The leadership pool grows. I've seen organizations where people refuse to seek promotion because they are already stressed at the level they are at now.

Whether you are a CEO, manager, executive director, school superintendent, pastor, or public official, when you recognize opportunities to operate more fully from the Spirit of Leadership, you build a stronger, people-focused organization. There are no profits when people are not the focus. Mergers and acquisitions suffer when people are not the focus. Service quality diminishes when people are not the focus. It's difficult to keep good staff and customers when people are not the focus. You can't even get elected when people are not the focus. You cannot use and abuse people and think you will sustain success. It is a sure path to failure. But when you commit to purposeful growth, people begin to see that being connected to you and your vision means growth for them.

BE FULLY PRESENT

Being fully present is the result of self-awareness. To be fully present means:

> *To be so immersed in the highest future potential of others*
> *that it increases their capacity to believe for what is possible.*

Being fully present is connecting to your *yes*. It is showing up in a state of future possibility. When you are with the people you lead and serve, you must engage with their greater Self. You speak to their greater Self. This is now a reality for you. This future is not far off. It is happening now, and it is becoming all at the same time.

Being fully present is not easy. It takes a lot of energy. Why? Because you have to force yourself to overcome your own limiting beliefs and behaviors. You have to undo all preconceived notions of a person or people. You're fully vested in their world. You are vulnerable in their world. You have to sometimes battle through the superficial to get to the core of their greatness.

The practice of being fully present is called "presencing." Dr. Otto Scharmer describes "presencing" as:

> *The blend of sensing and presence means to connect with*
> *the Source of the highest future possibility and to bring it*
> *into the now. When moving into the state of "presencing,"*
> *perception begins to happen from a future possibility that*
> *depends on us to come into reality. In that state we step*
> *into our real being, who we really are, our authentic self.* [8]

As the Leader, you are fully present and fully sensing at the same time. As a reminder, the Spirit of Leadership is the Convicting Power that moves us to say yes to the vision, work, and risk of making things remarkably better for others. There are four areas where the Leader must maintain self-awareness and be fully present:

---

8   Otto C. Scharmer, *Theory U: Leading from the Future as it Emerges* (Cambridge, USA: The Society for Organizational Learning, 2007).

1) Fully present with the Convicting Power.

2) Fully present with your yes.

3) Fully present with the vision, work, and risk.

4) Fully present with others.

> # When I think of Leaders who were fully present with the Convicting Power I think of Cesar Chavez.

FULLY PRESENT WITH THE CONVICTING POWER

Leading your organization forward is not just about who and what informs you but also what convicts you. The Convicting Power is the force that awakens you to a need that needs to be solved. Whether it is political, financial, or a social injustice, the Convicting Power visits you and says, "You need to pay attention to this. I need you to move toward it." And no matter what, you can't shake it. You become more and more aware of the issue. It becomes a part of your world. You don't feel right trying to ignore it. It's almost as if it is sitting there looking straight at you saying, "I'm not going to leave you alone until you do something about this!" The Convicting Power is that thing within you that keeps pushing you to do what you know is right. This means speaking up, letting people go, or taking the risk to go after big opportunities.

When I think of Leaders who were fully present with the Convicting Power I think of Cesar Chavez. Chavez founded the United Farm Workers of America (UFW). The UFW arose out of the need for better working conditions on farms and to serve as a rebuff for inhumane work treatment that included but was not limited to: subpar wages, lack of sanitation, no workplace protections, and a whole host of malfeasance. Mr. Chavez led this movement and won important victories to raise pay and improve working conditions for farm workers in the late 1960s and 1970s. Cardinal Roger Mahony, retired prelate of the Catholic Church, wrote about Chavez in a 1993 *LA Times* article, stating how everything Cesar did was underpinned by his faith.[9] His vision was energized by this spirituality.

Cesar Chavez had to learn that there are moments in Leadership when you must follow clarity and conviction over certainty and consensus. This is not easy to do, especially when people's lives or millions or even billions of dollars are at stake. Michael Dell knew this Convicting Power when he disappointed his parents by choosing to drop out of college to build his computer business. Bob Iger had to rely on this conviction when approaching Steve Jobs to buy Pixar which was outperforming Disney Studios by a longshot. Yet Iger had a gut feeling that he needed to make it happen, even though his inner circle tried to dissuade him[10]. Or maybe it's not money. Maybe it is about the freedom and equity for an underserved and underrepresented people group.

---

9   Roger Mahony, "A Voice of Justice, Following the Gospel: Cesar Chavez: His Faith and Commitment to Nonviolence Brought Dignity to Farm Workers Across the Southwest," *Los Angeles Times,* April 25, 1993, https://www.latimes.com/archives/la-xpm-1993-04-25-op-27069-story.html.
10   Bob Iger, *The Ride of a Lifetime: Lessons learned from 15 years as CEO of the Walt Disney Company* (New York: Random House, 2019).

Whether you are a CEO, entrepreneur, public sector leader, educator, or faith leader, there must be something motivating you to step up and move things forward. The Leader leaves behind revolutionary change. Those who are not committed to moving things forward are simply holding down a job and are no more than glorified task managers. If you feel you are called to be the Leader, then you have a purpose that you must fulfill. It is being fully present with the Convicting Power that gives you the ability to work beyond your natural strength and ability.

For the Leader, times will come when you want to quit, give up, and walk away from it all. You will face difficult times in your Leadership. You will feel alone and lonely. But at the end of the day, it's only the Convicting Power that pushes you to get back in the fight and move forward. Are you in tune with the Convicting Power?

Being fully present with this Convicting Power only speaks to what is possible. The Convicting Power shows you a compelling vision and asks you to sign up for it. This is tough because it cannot always be explained or put into words. It's that deep feeling within that pulls on your heart strings. Whether you believe in the God of the Bible or some other higher force, you and I both know that we are all guided by something or someone much bigger than life itself. During the tough times of your Leadership, when you feel that you bit off more than you can chew, you are going to need to rely on the fact that you didn't call yourself to be the Leader in the first place.

Leaders who are convicted by a Greater Power tend to inspire others to want to follow and work with them. The Convicting

Power is the force that draws the gifts, talents, and skills out of the Leader that he never knew he had (or maybe was afraid to tap into).

Cesar Chavez was once asked to explain how he had sustained himself over so many years of struggle. He responded, "I don't think I could base my will to struggle on cold economics or on some political doctrine. I don't think there would be enough to sustain me. For me, the base must be faith!"

And you, despite opposition, are willing to move toward what is unseen to the common eye. As you read these words, focus on your Leadership role. What is driving you to lead? Fame? Promotion? Money? Prestige? Or is it purpose, necessity, or transforming society?

FULLY PRESENT WITH YOUR YES

After yielding to the Convicting Power, the Leader simply says, "Yes." The Leaders we admire are often those who were bold enough to say yes to something that most people were afraid to. These leaders do not wait to be certain. They do not wait for consensus. They say yes and do their best to prepare for what is to come. For the Leader, saying yes is a defining moment. Everything changes from this point on. Saying yes changes the Leader's status. She rises above those who were once her peers and is now called to lead them. She is not controlled by anyone except her own commitment. She only answers to her yes. Your yes doesn't make you fearless per se, but it does make you fear less. While she may have a boss or board of directors, her yes points her to her true north. To be the Leader, you must be fully present with your yes. Your yes is not a job or position. Your yes is your cause. Your yes becomes your why. It is your reason for doing what you do in each moment, whether the moment is good or bad.

Cesar Chavez simply said Yes! He said yes to equitable treatment of migrant workers. In the face of many unfair "nos," he continued to say yes to the Convicting Power.

Your yes will often lead you through four stages of emotions and intellect:

1) *You're pissed.* Something you see becomes the straw that breaks the camel's back and you can no longer sit around and do nothing.

2) *You're Passionate.* You become connected to the possibility of change. Passion drives you to find solutions and helps you stay the course.

3) *You become more proficient.* Passion alone won't do it. You must increase in wisdom and knowledge. Wisdom invigorates your passion. You are now solution-focused.

4) *Your outcome is peace.* The result of the Leader is not more confusion, animosity, or dissension. The result is peace and harmony. The Leader always seeks to create situations and environments that make things remarkably better for others.

What is the yes for your Leadership? Are you showing up every day for a title or a position? Is your goal to climb the corporate ladder so you can tell others "Look what I did!" Or are you leading because something needs to change and you feel life prepared you for this moment? You weren't necessarily qualified to lead in the position you're in. You don't have the right credentials or experience. You haven't accumulated enough years of experience. No doubt, there are others who have much better qualifications on paper. But it's your yes that compels you to raise your hand or stand up and say, "I'll do it!" This is what it means to yield to and be fully present with your yes. To be aligned with your yes is the most fulfilling aspect of leading. Tough times will come, but your yes will remind you of why you are here. You will feel alone as the Leader. You will cry in your office. You'll want to give up at times, but your yes won't let you (and this is another reason you may cry). Consequently, if the Spirit of Leadership is the Convicting Power that moves us to say yes to the vision, work, and risk of making things remarkably better for others, then we also need to be aware of what we must say no to. Saying yes is saying no.

FULLY PRESENT WITH THE VISION, WORK, AND RISK

As we yield our yes to the vision, work, and risk, we must also be self-aware of the work we're saying yes to. The work requires creativity and innovation. The Convicting Power would never move you to the work just to keep it status quo. America's founding fathers were fully present with the vision, work, and risk of making the United States of America remarkably better for its new and future citizens.

They had a vision for progress and growth and understood that this was essential for building a thriving nation. They knew that complacency would hinder the realization of their vision. Along with their vision, they committed to a work that demanded tremendous dedication, resilience, and innovation. Their commitment to shaping a nation founded on principles of freedom, democracy, and equality empowered their determination to overcome challenges and move forward despite the uncertainties and risks of the time.

Leaders who are fully present with the vision, work, and risk are often criticized for their intense focus on achieving the intended results. Because of their self-awareness of the Convicting Power and their yes, they know the sacrifices that their team will need to make. The journey is sometimes hard and takes a deeper level of commitment from others. Still the Leader does whatever he can to develop his team for the work and risk. Cesar Chavez, who committed to vision, work, and risk of leading a non-violent movement, also had to witness violence against his followers. Many people died because of their commitment to the vision, work, and risk of getting Mexican farm workers equal pay. I am not saying that you have to risk people losing their lives when you lead. I am saying that, as the Leader, you have to move forward regardless of the risk you and your team will face.

The people who work for you, those who receive a weekly, bi-weekly, or monthly paycheck, have families who are depending on you to make the right decisions and keep the organization profitable so they can maintain their lifestyles. This is the risk you take as the Leader. You need to be fully present with the vision, work, and risk. Always know where you're going and what the next big win must be. You may not always know the steps to take but stay focused on the destination. Patrick Lencioni reminds us that Leaders must create clarity, overcommunicate clarity, and then reinforce clarity.

FULLY PRESENT WITH OTHERS

Bottom line, Leadership is all about people. If the result of Leadership is to make things remarkably better for others, then we ought to pay close attention to the needs and insights of those we lead and serve. This is external or public self-awareness.

Self-awareness is not only gained by the information you tell yourself; more importantly, it is gained by the insights gathered from those you lead and serve and those in your inner circle. The Leader cannot be dismissive of what others think about him. A true Leader seeks this information. To be the Leader, you must frequently ask others questions that reveal how they see you. The challenge of this is that most people are not always sure they can tell their leader how they really feel. They usually tell the leader what she wants to hear for fear of reprisal or being terminated.

Being fully present in these four areas will always bring you back to the internal indicators mentioned in chapter one:

- Being fully present with the Convicting Power centers you with the Global Vision.
- Being fully present with your yes ignites within you the inexplicable faith and conviction to do something now.
- Being fully present with the vision, work, and risk ignites a willingness to make the sacrifice and move forward.
- Being fully present with others ignites a passion to see others win.

Caesar Chavez said:

"I am convinced that the truest act of courage, the strongest act of manliness, is to sacrifice ourselves for others in a totally non-violent struggle for justice," Chavez

*declared, in a speech read on his behalf when his first
hunger strike ended. "To be a man is to suffer for others.
God help us be men."*

When you invest your time and attention to being self-aware
and fully present, you not only transform your own life but you
also transform those around you. Each conversation, each interaction becomes an opportunity to plant seeds of empathy, understanding, and kindness. As these seeds take root and flourish, the
impact ripples outward, creating an environment that empowers
others to succeed.

HOW BEING SELF-AWARE AND FULLY
PRESENT EMPOWERS OTHERS

If your organization acts like you, then being a self-aware and
fully present Leader means having an organization that knows
its potential and works hard to get there. The key to being fully
present is tapping into the human spirit. The human spirit is the
core of a person's being. The peace, joy, and love of God dwells
in this core. It is also the place where faith, expectation, passion,
and determination live. The presence of the human spirit is the
reason why human beings desire to be and do more. It is more
real than our physical nature. It sees what is impossible for the
human eye to see. It believes beyond reality. It has no limits. The
human spirit is only hindered by the unbelief of the carnal mind,
but once it is released, it becomes unstoppable. The human spirit
is a person's fully manifested potential. It is housed internally but
has not been released externally. This is the place where we are
most divine. It is the area of our lives where we are motivated and

inspired. Whenever an individual's human spirit is empowered, her hope is restored and her dreams don't seem impossible. It may not be seen on the outside, but it is alive on the inside. So it is the Leader's main job to awaken this sleeping giant so that the individual can experience her best life. When these two are activated simultaneously, you awaken your superhuman power to unleash the greatness in others.

> ## As the Leader you must train your spirit to hear the words that can't be articulated.

The key for me to succeed in any talk or speech is not solely in what I have to say, but it is in how I engage my audience. It rests in how I allow them to see through me as I'm on stage and how complete I see them from the stage. For me, to be present means to speak in a way where the person in the back row feels that they are sitting in Starbucks with me having a Strawberry Acai with Lemonade (my favorite drink).

"Presencing" is not just about eye contact. It is more about spirit contact. How well do I communicate to the part of the human that says no words and makes no sound, but pierces the heart with its silent declarations? It's the foundation that enables us to hear what's not being said. As the Leader you must train your spirit to hear the words that can't be articulated. You have to discern pains that can't be uttered in a language. Engaging those you lead is not academic; it can't be learned through a process.

You need to know this as the Leader who transforms those you lead and serve.

To see the full humanness of those we lead and serve is a Divine gift. We are most effective when we can tap into the inner self and call forth what lies dormant within a person. This spiritual wonder can live in multiple dimensions at the same time, whereas the physical nature is limited only to the present. The human spirit reveals to you hope, ignites your faith, and will cause you to press on even though your present situation is opposite of what your human spirit has revealed. It takes a Leader or an agent of change to help a person unlock this highly untapped area of our lives.

To be self-aware and fully present means you must:

1) Enter their world.

2) Learn from their viewpoint.

3) Identify with their experience (empathy).

4) Speak to their strength.

5) Be their strength.

As you explore their world, you see greater opportunities to lead and get the best out of them.

Many leaders do not invest significant time in their Leadership growth and development. They measure leadership success by how well they survived the chaos or endured the pressure from the board.

Many organizations we've worked with do not have a Leadership development program. The leaders in place are those who can pass a test. Or maybe they're the ones who can manage the chaos better than others and keep showing up to work every day without complaining. These organizations rarely choose leaders who can move the organization forward. They don't invest in Leaders who are natural disruptors. As a matter of fact, they often shun these types of Leaders or fire them simply because they just need a leader who can manage what already is without breaking it or making it worse. If a person can do that well, then they get to lead. But this is not Leadership. And therefore, these organizations and companies are rarely known for doing anything great.

At the end of the day, these potential Leaders end their careers never achieving the level of greatness that they could have. They retire or get fired having worked hard and all people can say about them is, "Well, at least they didn't drive us out of business!" This is not fair to that Leader nor the people they get to lead. Therefore, the Leader doesn't get the opportunity to judge his leadership by growth and innovation, but by maintenance and preservation. In this, the leader needs opportunities to discover who he is as a Leader. He will never get the opportunity to come face-to-face with who he can be when operating as a leader who maintains and preserves. This is not to say that these leaders are not amazing people. I am not saying that people don't want to follow and work with them. I am simply saying that even if this leader has wings, the managing, maintaining, and preserving work prohibits them from finding the wind that helps them fly and soar higher.

When your leadership is only ascribed to maintenance and preserving, it is difficult to be fully present with those you lead and serve. I have met many leaders who would love to spend time developing their leaders but are often sucked into a meeting or putting out a fire.

THE ENEMIES OF BEING SELF-AWARE AND FULLY PRESENT

You want to be the Leader. But if you're honest, competing priorities, corporate politics, meeting after meetings (when it could have been said in an email), and other ever-changing vicissitudes of the job keep you from becoming the Leader you know you are called to be. You are convinced there is so much more that you could do. There's more you could offer and more you can become. But the structure has been created to keep you busy managing things and not leading people. This leaves you feeling stuck and unfulfilled. Being too busy to grow in self-awareness and and being fully present creates distance between the people you lead and serve. Burnout increases. People don't feel psychologically safe anymore. The return on the gift of being self-aware and fully present is increased performance, productivity, and quality of work. Too many leaders are only defined by how well they can juggle multiple tasks. It's not really about did you become a better leader more than it is did you survive and not negatively impact the organization. Even with all of the chaos, board members, directs, and stakeholders, expect a leader to get things done. No excuses. And they should perform and get things done. But leaders must also make time to develop themselves. In his book *Hidden Truths*, David Fubini talks about the rigor that new executives often face. They begin with a big vision. In the beginning they are ready to change the world. However, they quickly see that the job pushes them into the busyness of work. But if the leader doesn't invest in herself, then the team will rarely take time to invest in themselves and will ultimately find another job that values professional development. [11]

> # Whether an organization is healthy, dysfunctional, or stuck, it always acts like its leader.

Remember, whether your organization is healthy, dysfunctional, or stuck, it always acts like its leader. Therefore, your organization often becomes a reflection of who you really are.

Being a self-aware and fully present Leader sets the tone for the kind of organization you want to build. It positions you to go beyond the superficial attributes of authority and move deeper into understanding how to inspire people from their highest future potential to where they are now. You no longer have a set Leadership style. You are not bound by a personality trait that cannot be broken. Instead, you learn how to be malleable, adjusting to the hopes and needs of your team without ever losing the essence of who you really are. You develop situational awareness and no matter the moment or challenge, you can become the Leader people need you to be to help them get to the next level. Having this sense of self elevates you into a realm of Leadership

---

11 David Fubini, Hidden *Truths: What Leaders Need to Hear But Are Rarely Told* (Hoboken, New Jersey: John Wiley & Sons, Inc., 2020).

very few occupy. You no longer require people to adapt to you. You adapt to and become fully present with the Convicting Power that drives you to say yes. It is your yes that draws out the kind of Leader you will be.

This heightened awareness allows for a harmonious symphony of collaboration, where more people feel they are valued, and they matter. By being a self-aware and fully present Leader, you begin the journey of establishing an environment where people begin to willingly trust you, trust your Leadership, and trust your ability to lead them to the vision.

CHAPTER 3

EARN THEIR TRUST, RESPECT, AND CONFIDENCE

When one of my clients was hired as CEO, she came to this organization highly sought after. Her resume was very impressive. Before taking this role, she had worked with various heads of state from countries around the world, helping them to advance their state initiatives and programs. Christine (not her real name) had a knack for bringing high-profile figures together and getting them to invest millions into projects. But once she was hired as CEO, the pressure began. She was used to working with people on a short-term project basis. Six months here, twelve months there, and then she moved on to another project. She was so good at her work that she was always in demand.

The previous CEO had left the organization and the board was looking for a dynamic Leader to move the organization to the next level. The board hired Christine because of her extraordinary ability to cast a compelling vision and her expertise in making connections with influencers and business leaders. They were confident that she was the executive to get the organization more recognition in their region. But eventually, the problems arose the moment she got there.

While Christine was excellent in project management, raising money, and networking, she was now in a role that required a different skillset. She was there to lead people, not be a consultant. The people she was to lead were not going to leave after six or twelve months. Many had already been working in the organization for more than fifteen years. She was not there to fix one problem and move on. Christine had committed herself to serving as CEO for at least three years. But the issues began on day one.

Christine's biggest issue was engaging her new board and team. People would hire her for her expertise. She did not have to spend as much time building relationships. This is one area Christine lacked. As the new CEO, she was a "here's what needs to be done, now let's go do it!" kind of leader. Now, this is not necessarily a bad approach to leading others. I am not saying that the Leader does not have to lead with urgency at some point. But this is not a long-game approach. And this only works best when the Leader has earned the trust, respect, and confidence of the people he leads and serves.

I received a call from Christine about one year into her CEO role. The number one challenge we had to work through was how to relate to her board. Of course, there were issues with her staff as well. There were conflicts with her managers and their teams. Before Christine called me, she was already writing up a manager and was about to let her go, but the manager eventually quit. The staff would bypass Christine and complain to the board about her behavior.

In our first conversation, Christine felt everyone was against her. She could not see the part she played in the conflict. She told me that she was just trying to do what the board asked her to do. She felt she needed to improve the work ethic, get people focused on doing their job, and then grow the organization's revenue. These are definitely things the Leader should focus on. But the Leader knows there is something that proceeds this. The Leader knows that she must first earn, trust, respect, and confidence with the people she leads and serves.

You have the vision. You have the right strategy. But until you earn people's trust, respect, and confidence, you won't be able to move your organization or initiative forward. Being the Leader is not just about getting people to follow what you say. Being the Leader is about earning enough of people's trust respect, and confidence to get them to see what is possible, collaborate as a team, and commit and contribute to achieving the vision. We no longer live in a "do what I say, not as I do" time. More than ever, people need proof. If you had to rate yourself on a scale of 1-5 (5 being the highest), how would you rate your team's trust, respect, and confidence when it comes to your Leadership?

Earning trust, respect, and confidence is more about giving value to the people you lead and serve. You are the Leader, but you do not hold that over them. You do not show up proving you are the Leader. The person who feels they have to prove they are the Leader is not the Leader. They are insecure and need to grow up. No one has to respect you because you are the Leader. The CEO or executive title is not a criterion for earning trust, respect, and confidence. The big corner office nor the executive salary and package gives you permission to demand trust, respect, and confidence. What positions you to earn trust, respect, and confidence is that you serve others well.

The Gift we give to others when we earn trust, respect, and confidence is a gift that says, "You have value and worth. You matter to me."

Earning trust, respect, and confidence is simply based on you consistently offering the gift of Leadership to them in the most personal and meaningful way possible.

When I coach Leaders, I do my best to help them recognize opportunities to operate more fully from the Spirit of Leadership. This can be difficult at times because leaders are often trying to figure out how to manage chaos and keep their job. They rarely make it a priority to lead in a way that earns trust, respect, and confidence. But it is so important for leaders to break out of this mentality so they can be the Leader that people love to follow and work with.

ANSWER THE THREE QUESTIONS

The people you lead are watching your every move. There is a meter that they use to determine the level of commitment and contribution they will give to your vision. They use this meter to judge the decisions you make, how you plan, how you communicate, how you treat others, how you execute, and how well you display emotional intelligence in conflict. This meter that people use to judge your Leadership is based on three questions. These questions determine the amount of energy people will give to following you and supporting your vision. The three questions that your team asks are:

1) Do I believe what you are saying?
2) How will I benefit (personally and professionally) from following you?
3) Can I trust you to lead me there?

When you consistently answer these questions in a way that inspires belief, you earn the people's trust, respect, and confidence. The moment you default on either one of these questions, red flags rise and commitment diminishes. People may never verbally ask these questions of Leaders, but please know, as the Leader, you must still answer them in your performance. Throughout every stage of Leadership, the people you lead and serve are asking these three questions. And you must answer all three. Here is how the Leader might approach these questions.

DO PEOPLE BELIEVE WHAT YOU ARE SAYING?

In order to earn trust, respect, and confidence from the people you lead and serve, they must first believe in what you have to say. To be believable, simply tell the truth. Always tell the truth. Never lie. Never deceive the people you lead and serve. Getting people to believe you is not a three-step program. There are no tactics or gimmicks to make people believe you. Getting people to believe you is simply about being a person of integrity. In his book, *The Speed of Trust: The One Thing That Changes Everything*, Stephen M.R. Covey writes, "A person has integrity when there is no gap between intent and behavior . . . when he or she is whole, seamless, the same—inside and out."[12]

> In order to earn trust, respect, and confidence from the people you lead and serve, they must first believe in what you have to say.

Integrity increases the speed of trust. Before people trust you as the Leader, they must first trust you as a person. The more integrity in your everyday life, the easier it is to gain trust. People want to see you as a person, as a parent, as a spouse, and as a human being. You cannot have integrity as the Leader but then fail to have integrity as a parent or spouse. This impacts the trust people have in you. It does not mean you cannot regain their trust, but it definitely impacts people's trust, respect, and confidence in you.

People will follow you and increase their performance and productivity when they have a Leader with a high level of integrity in their personal and professional life. Integrity helps people believe the vision or plan you are setting before them. Whenever you speak about what is to come or where you desire to take the organization, you want their response to be, "I can see us doing

---

12 Stephen M.R. Covey, *The Speed of Trust: The One Thing That Changes Everything* (New York: Free Press, 2008).

that," "Wow, I want to be a part of that," or maybe even, "This is a scary step, but we have to do this!"

We tend to believe someone when they awaken hope and cause us to see a pathway to a better life that we had not yet considered. People believe through their senses. If they can touch it, feel it, see it, hear it, smell it, or even sense something strongly within their heart, they are more influenced to believe it is true. To do this you must reduce their fear and induce their faith. People believe what the Leader is saying when the Leader can convince them:

- That the challenge is not as hard as it seems.
- That the people are much bigger than the challenge they face.
- That the people deserve better and should fight for it, even though it's hard.

If the Leader can do these three things while maintaining integrity, compassion, and empathy for others, then this will open the door for people to give you their trust, respect, and confidence. This all comes from the Spirit of Leadership. People begin to believe in your yes. They sense that you are all in and have committed to the vision, work, and risk of making things remarkably better for them.

HOW WILL OTHERS BENEFIT?

People know they will benefit when they see that you consider others in your planning and decision-making. If a leader is making decisions and people do not feel they were considered in that decision, the people will not support her. But when the Leader gets input from the people, listens to the people, and plans for the people, then the people will increase their buy-in.

Humility is the key to being the Leader that ensures the process and outcome will benefit others. Humility is the fine line between insecurity and arrogance. The Leader knows her strength and power but does not flaunt it. She is self-aware of her greatness and ability to lead yet she shows up as a servant. She is meek. I once heard that meekness means strength under control. Being a humble Leader reminds you that people are important, they have a hope and a future, and their input matters. Being humble helps us to make room for others. We give people space and invite them to belong.

Remember, your focus as the Leader is to make things remarkably better for others. Your Leadership is a gift for them. What do people get by following you? How will they be better by following you? How will they benefit from saying yes to your vision? How might their lives change by saying yes to the work? Think about the risks involved. What benefit will one receive by taking on these risks with you? People need a guarantee. Give your team insurance and assurance that through your Leadership, they will grow and achieve great things by working together. People follow you at the speed of your genuine compassion and care. They don't mind being pushed, as long as it's with your heart and not your fist.

When I think of someone who leads to benefit others, I am reminded of author, consummate educator, and my mentor, Dr. Judy White. In every Leadership position she held, she made room for others to thrive. She coached them, mentored them, and trained them. Dr. White knew that she was called to rise through the ranks of K-12 education. She also knew that the greatest reflection of her Leadership was determined by how many Leaders she created and helped promote.

Whenever she received a promotion, she brought people with her and promoted them too. Dr. White was not concerned about receiving the spotlight. She knew her promotions were fruitless without also helping others rise. She brought on rising stars and encouraged them to do better than she had. Many of these Leaders are now leading school districts, serving as state Leaders in education, and many have stepped out and launched their own businesses.

I must admit that I would not be where I am today if not for Dr. White. I was just launching BEK Impact Corp. in 2017 when Dr. White was promoted to become the Superintendent of Riverside County Office of Education. She gave me my first contract that lasted two years. By being connected to Dr. White, our company generated more than $450,000 over a four-year period. It is an age-old principle that when you do good for others, good will happen for you. My favorite book, the Bible, tells us that when we "... humble ourselves under the might power of God ... at the right time he will lift you up in honor."[13]

Become what I call, the "Helium Leader." Your Leadership, communication, and engagement should cause others to rise higher, simply because they had an encounter with you. Do your best to be the source that makes everyone around you better. Even when times are tough, practice being the Helium Leader. The harder the task, the more time you need to spend with those you lead and serve. The more energy draining the work or project, the more your team will need to be encouraged and inspired by you. If you have done all you can to help a staff member and still must let him go, be the Helium Leader and let him know you believe in him.

---

13 1 Peter 5:6 (New Living Translation)

CAN PEOPLE TRUST YOU TO LEAD THEM?

Okay. So you have given your team a vision that they believe in. And you have convinced them that this vision will benefit them. But now you must convince them that you are the Leader to take them from here to there. It is one thing for people to believe what you say, but it is another thing for them to believe that you can lead them.

To earn your team's trust in your Leadership, they must see that you are all in with one thing: your yes to the vision, work, and risk of making things remarkably better for others.

When a client of mine, Tyreese (not his real name and the details of the story have been altered to protect everyone) was new to his executive leadership role, he was able to convince the board that he had a great vision. He also was able to convey the organizational benefits for both board and staff. So the board hired him. Soon after, the problems began to surface. It was not long before Tyreese hired me as his coach. He told me he felt it was his job to "clean house," and get rid of the people who were under the previous executive leader. So he made it hard on everyone.

Tyreese was hired because he was great at raising money. At the time he came aboard, the organization's revenue had floundered quite a bit, so the board was eager to hire an executive who could correct this deficiency. Tyreese was the perfect fit for raising money but struggled to lead the people. As the board began to notice Tyreese's lack of Leadership, they began to reject many of Tyreese's ideas. They eventually rejected a budget Tyreese had submitted. Tyreese was not a selfish person. He simply struggled making his yes more about others than himself.

The people he led did not feel Tyreese would fight for them. He often fussed at them when they did not do things the way he wanted them done. Tyreese was also notorious for not being prepared when it came to meeting deadlines. He would often put the pressure on the staff to "hurry and get this done," and if they could not, he would come down hard on them.

I could go on and on, but I think you get the point. Tyreese was able to communicate a clear, compelling vision and show how others would benefit, but he failed to commit to a yes that made things remarkably better for others. Our coaching sessions were tough. I cannot say that Tyreese has done a total 180-degree change. We did see some progress in certain areas, but unfortunately, the board let Tyreese go. He called me early one morning to tell me the news. I was hurt. I wasn't only hurt because Tyreese was let go, but also because he could not see the role he played in being fired. Tyreese seemed to struggle with the concept of earning trust, respect, and confidence. Even in the end, he was so engrossed in what he wanted for the organization that he continued to blame the board and his executive team for not seeing things his way. I tried to help him to understand that getting people on board with your vision begins with trust. They have to trust you in order for you to lead them. Tyreese managed the process, but failed to lead the people. No one on the team felt Tyreese was for them. They felt he was a task master. And because of this they never offered him their trust and commitment.

When people know that you will fight for them, stand with them, stand up for them, move with them, make the way, and lead the way, they will be more inclined to allow you to lead them. People want to follow and work with the Leader who will involve herself in matters that have seemingly no relevance to her except for the fact that the matter affects those she leads and loves. This is the summum bonum of the Leader's quest to earn trust, respect, and confidence.

> When people know that you will fight for them, stand with them, stand up for them, move with them, make the way, and lead the way, they will be more inclined to allow you to lead them.

So what if you are a new Leader and no one knows you? If you want people to believe you, understand that they probably won't just jump right in at first. You have to earn it. I often encourage Leaders to put themselves on a trial or probationary plan and let their team know. Ask them to enroll in your plan but with a "money-back guarantee." Give them incentives for joining you. Ask them what indicators they would like to see. The journey has to be about showing that you are a person whose words and actions match. As you build upon this and remain consistent, people will believe you a little more and their performance, productivity, and quality of work will improve.

Ultimately, people need to trust that you have the expertise, knowledge, and ability to lead them to a goal, but they also need to see your sacrifice. You must assure them that you will not bail on them when things get hard. They must feel that you will go to bat for them.

THE BENEFITS OF EARNING TRUST

Your vision is important. Your strategy is important. The organization's culture is important. But you will never get the best from your team until they can trust you. Covey states that trust is the:

> . . . one thing which, if removed, will destroy the most powerful government, the most successful business, the most thriving economy, the most influential leadership, the greatest friendship, the strongest character, the deepest love. On the other hand, if developed and leveraged, that one thing has the potential to create unparalleled success and prosperity in every dimension of life. [14]

Trust is the foundation of a team. Trust is like the couplers that hold train cars together. A coupler requires extraordinary strength. It must be able to handle the hills, dips, and curves that trains endure on their journey to their destination. If a coupler is not strong, if it fails to properly connect to the other cars that

---

14 Covey, *The Speed of Trust*.

make the train, then great damage will come to the train and most importantly, the people inside of it.

This is what trust is to the Leader and his team. Trust is the coupler that connects the team to each other and to the Leader. When the trust is strong, they are able to endure hills, dips, valleys, and curves, and still remain together. They can go through dark tunnels and maintain unity. No one has their own agenda. Everyone is heading in the same direction. Even when someone does not know what to do, they know that, because they are connected as a team, the team will help them get to where it is they need to go.

In his book *The Five Dysfunctions of a Team*, Patrick Lencioni writes how trust is about vulnerability. It allows teams to be comfortable expressing their opinions without fear of ridicule or feeling less than. They can admit that they were wrong or that they do not know the answer.[15] People are free to share ideas, even if they sound crazy. This kind of vulnerability establishes trust to draw out the best from the people on the team. It is a gift that says to them, "You belong here."

Now, here's my big ask: please reconsider leading people if you struggle being a Leader who is trustworthy and has integrity. Make no mistake about it. You hire them because of their character and competency. But they hire you because they can trust your Leadership.

While there are some leaders who have succeeded at pulling the wool over people's eyes, history tells us that these leaders are soon found out. It is difficult to be who you are not. The Bible states, "A double minded man is unstable in all of his ways." [16]

---

15 Patrick Lencioni, *The Five Dysfunctions of a Team* (Winsome Book India, 2009).
16 James 1:8 (King James Version)

It is difficult to manage two conflicting characters at once. One will eventually take over the other, and it is usually the one that negatively impacts people's trust, respect, and confidence. A bucking horse can try to convince me all it wants that it is a strong, powerful animal, but I will never trust it to give me a ride. Why? Because I know its character.

THE BENEFITS OF EARNING RESPECT

You have heard it said many times: Respect is earned, not given. This means that if you want people to respect you, then you must first respect them. Leaders give respect to those they lead and serve. However, the Leader does not give respect because he wants to earn respect. The Leader does not walk into a room and say, "I need people to respect me so let me respect them first!" Giving respect is a lifestyle for the Leader. This lifestyle is embedded in the Spirit of Leadership. The Leader is not focused on giving respect to earn respect. The Leader gives respect because it is the humane thing to do. Leaders do not stop respecting others when they are disrespected. They stay the course and continue to respect. The outcome for giving respect is that you gave respect, not that you earned respect in return. The Leader never feels he deserves respect simply because he is the Leader. He knows he earns respect by consistently leading from the Spirit of Leadership.

Your goal for giving respect is not to get people to respect you. As Leaders, we should never give with the expectation of receiving something for ourselves. This is a self-centered, insecure approach. As the Leader, you give because it adds value to those you lead and serve. You give because it empowers them to achieve their personal and professional goals. Leaders respect people because it is one of the most honorable things to do. When people feel empowered by the Leader, they give more to the work they are doing in return. When they see themselves growing and achieving more, they tend to offer even more respect to the one who empowered them.

Getting respect is not the goal. The goal is respecting others in a way that shows you are fully present with who they are now and who they are becoming. Receiving respect is often the byproduct of the goal. Respect allows the Leader to connect with people at the most human level. He wants to show the people he leads and serves that he is respectful and that he will do his best to always respect their greatness and human spirit. And when they believe this, he will eventually earn their trust, respect, and confidence in his Leadership.

Leaders must avoid asking, "How do I get people to like me?" or, "How do I get people to respect me?" Instead, they should ask, "How can I give my very best and get the best out of them?" Remember, the gift is not for you. The gift is for them. Leaders do not respect people to get respect. Leaders respect people because it is the right thing to do.

THE BENEFITS OF EARNING CONFIDENCE

You're probably pretty confident that when you sit down on a chair it will hold you up. Whether you sit in a chair in a restaurant, an office, or a church building, you normally would not expect it to break from under you. When go to sit down, you don't wonder if the chair is stable enough to hold you up. You just sit. Why? Because chairs are meant and built to hold you up. You have seen many times that chairs hold people up. It has consistent results in doing so. Therefore you are confident to walk in a room, pull out a chair, and just sit down on it. As a matter of fact, you'd be shocked if the chair didn't hold you up. And so should your Leadership be. People should be confident that, in the best of times and in the worst of times, they can lean on you to lead them and not have your integrity or character or will to lead them forward break under pressure. The people you lead and serve will increase confidence in your Leadership as you remain stable and consistent, continue to serve them well, and are willing to lead from the front and make the necessary sacrifices along the way.

Tom and Heather Flores, lead pastors of Elevate Life Church in Riverside, CA, are probably two of the most sacrificial Leaders I know. I have known Tom and Heather since 2015. My family has attended many services at the church, and I speak there frequently. If the word sacrifice had a picture next to it, no doubt you would see the beautiful faces of Tom and Heather Flores. Even with a well-attended church of two thousand, the Flores' can still be found greeting people as they flood in for Sunday worship service. They work in the food pantry boxing up food for those who need it. You can find the Flores' going into homeless shelters, visiting the sick in the hospital, and cleaning the buildings they occupy (inside and out).

When the Flores' cast a vision, one thing the church members know is that they will be leading from the front. The church's donors believe in them because Tom and Heather lead from the front. People believe more in what they see you do than what they hear you say. To be believable, you simply have to do what you say you are going to do and be the first to make the sacrifice. Now, you may not be in the same industry as the Flores', but consider what sacrificial Leadership might look like in your organization. If your team were to say, "We have a sacrificial Leader," what might that mean to them? When Leaders sacrifice their time, talent, and resources for the sake of making things remarkably better for others, this raises the standard of Leadership in the entire organization. No one can say it cannot be done. They can see the Leader doing it. Sacrificial Leadership inspires others to give, be, and do their best.

> Great Leaders cast vision
> so big and convincing that
> their team begins to believe
> they can and increases their
> performance and productivity.

The Leader loses no credibility by not knowing, only by being unwilling to find out. Let them know that the journey includes detours, pivots, and sometimes throwing away the original plan as you learn and grow. Tough times will come. Strategies won't always work out as planned. There will be setbacks. As General

Oliver Prince Smith said as he commanded the 1st Marine Division during the Battle of Chosin Reservoir, "Retreat, hell! We're not retreating, we're just advancing in a different direction."

As you lead and help others succeed, you make deposits into their trust, respect, and confidence account.

People do not leave jobs; they leave a leader who is no longer able to answer the three questions. When a leader ceases to show their team what is possible, then top performers look elsewhere. Great Leaders cast vision so big and convincing that their team begins to believe they can and increases their performance and productivity.

——— CHAPTER 4 ———

GIVE THEM SOMETHING TO BELIEVE IN

The Leader's most powerful force is having a clear, compelling vision. Please know that people do not follow you. People follow what they believe they will become by following your vision. This is the gift. Within your Leadership is their future. The Leader who casts a great vision is one who exposes people to a future they didn't know existed or didn't believe was possible. Their future emerges through your Leadership.

Jesus made one of the most prolific statements in Matthew. He said, "Follow me, and I will make you fishers of men."[17] Jesus was quite assured that whoever followed Him would grow and increase. This is how confident He was in His vision. To Him it was simple: if they follow my vision, they will be better. And this is what you must solve as well:

Your vision + them following your vision = Makes them

_____.

What will you put in the blank space? The end result of following your vision is that people are made into something better

---

17 Matthew 4:19 (KJV)

than they are now. They follow, you make. Your vision makes people better. Vision inspires people to follow.

I could tell you of some amazing historical figures who cast a vision that inspired hundreds of thousands of people to follow and sacrifice for. Many I have already mentioned earlier. However, I want to share a moment that I was honored to be a part of. It was the launching of a vision (you might even call it a movement) for a company that (as of 2022) generates more than nine figures in revenue each year. I can vividly remember the night that Patrick Bet-David cast his vision for a new insurance marketing company called People Helping People, Inc. (PHP). I received a call around 8:00 p.m. from my director telling me one of the top leaders in our organization wanted to see the entire team. But wait. It's 8:00 p.m. and it would take me more than ninety minutes to drive from my house to the office in Woodland Hills, CA. Nevertheless, I made the drive because my director said it was urgent. I arrived to a full room of about 200 people. Most of the agents there were looking at each other trying to see if anyone knew why we were there. Most in the room had to drive quite a distance to get to the office. I kept asking my director what in the world was so important that couldn't be said over the phone? He said nothing.

Long story short, Patrick comes out and sits on a stool in the front of the room. It was there that he tells us that he is leaving the company and starting his own company. At this point, mouths have dropped to the floor. Patrick Bet-David founded PHP in 2009. In less than ten years, the company grew to a nine-figure business. I can remember him telling us that this would be the riskiest move for many who dared to follow.

He let everyone know that he had poured his entire savings into making this new business work. He also let us know that there was a high probability that this venture would not work and whoever followed him could lose everything. Patrick did not give anyone in the room money, incentives, a stake in the company, or any other material substance to entice us. He simply gave us a vision. A compelling vision. This was his gift to us that late night.

It was a gift that told us that greatness is often hidden in making bold, risky moves. It inspired us to look at our lives and wonder what else is possible. While many of us were doing well with the current company, many wondered, "Why not?" Why not take this leap and see what is on the other side?

That is what a great vision does. It inspires people to wonder what else is possible.

> When everyone has an opportunity to add value to the vision, their identity is invested into it. The vision is now not only a part of what they do, but who they are.

I once sat with a CEO and his executive team, helping them revise their vision, mission, and values and then operationalize it through their leadership, systems, and practice. While speaking to the team, I realized that too many organizations experience silos or get stuck because they only see the vision as a statement. A vision isn't a statement. A vision is a personality. It is who your organization is becoming. Vision has disciplines, behaviors, and a language. Vision has an attitude and an identity. Vision is also particular in declaring what it needs to manifest. Leaders must pay close attention to their vision.

The Leader does not hold anything back when communicating a vision. She wants the people she leads and serves to know, with all clarity, what the vision is, the work that everyone must do, and the risk associated with the work. Leaders should never be afraid or intimidated to invite their team into the vision development process. When everyone has an opportunity to add value to the vision, their identity is invested into it. The vision is now not only a part of what they do, but who they are.

Great Leaders have a unique way of helping their teams see themselves bigger and the task smaller, manageable, and easily accomplishable with the help and support of other big teammates and Leaders. Leaders only lead with their teams in the natural, but in vision, they are much further ahead. You succeed as the Leader when the frontline workers can speak the vision as if they created it.

IT'S YOUR JOB TO BELIEVE IT'S POSSIBLE

Whenever I coach Leaders, I'll ask them, "What do you want to achieve from our coaching sessions?" 99.999999% of the time they begin to tell me what they don't want. They will say, "Barry, you know our company has been dealing with [X] for a while now. Our numbers are down. Our teams are dysfunctional. We're busy, but we're just not making the impact that we want to make. If you can just help us get out of this rut we're in . . ."

After listening to them list their challenges, I ask, "Okay, when you're out of that rut, when X has been solved, then what else is possible for your organization? What will you do to stand out in your industry?" After I've asked this a few times, they usually stop and look at me with a blank stare and say, "Barry, you know what? I don't know."

It is human nature to focus more on what is wrong than what is possible. Regardless of the issue that people are facing, people tend to focus more on what they don't want instead of what they want to achieve. I have found that so many leaders are inundated, even overwhelmed with the busyness of work. Things are coming at them so fast. They are trying to manage the competing priorities and manage this team's issues and this team's problem. They have to get a report out and their Leadership is basically defined by what's happening in the now. The board meeting that they're in, the email that they have to respond to, and the presentation that they have to prepare.

They are so involved with managing tasks that they rarely get a chance to focus on what's next for their organization and how they can lead their teams there. So success to them is leading to not lose, not leading to win. If this is what your leadership looks like, you must break this limited thinking now.

The book of Numbers, my favorite book of the Bible, tells a story of twelve spies who went to spy on a very prosperous land that God was going to give to them. The twelve spies went in to spy on the land. When they returned back to the camp, ten of the spies gave an unfavorable report. Yes, they saw the land was prosperous and would be a great place to live, but there were giants living there too.

The twelve spies all saw the same land and that it was a very prosperous land, but not all twelve spies had the same vision. Ten of the spies had limited thinking. They came back and said, "We seemed like grasshoppers…IN OUR OWN EYES!"[18] They ultimately rejected and resisted the vision of going into the Promised Land. However, Caleb and Joshua had a different vantage point. They saw the land—the vision—and they came back and said, "WE CAN DO THIS!" (author paraphrase) How is it that two of the spies saw something totally different than the other ten? Because…

"You don't see things as 'they' are; you see things as you are!"

You cannot outperform your most dominant belief about yourself. Your vision disciplines belief. You become the image you see within. You have heard it said, "You become what you think about most of the time" or "As a man thinks, so he is!" It won't always make sense, but it still can be done.

Often our limiting beliefs and behaviors become our biggest hurdles to manifesting our vision. We can also get in our own way (or our team's) and not even realize how we're contributing to the problem we want to solve. So be careful to look at how your actions, comments, or leadership style impacts and affects others, even yourself.

As I have stated before, people don't follow you, they follow who they believe they can become by committing and working

---

18 Numbers 13:33 (New International Version)

toward the vision you stated. Your vision must be compelling enough to help people see themselves bigger and better. Vision is a gift that says, "This is for you."

To lead effectively, you must inspire your team to:

- See the vision.
- Believe the vision.
- Work hard for the vision.

They won't work hard if they don't believe it and they can't believe it if you do not help them see it.

Having a clear, compelling vision that you believe in is important for Leadership. It is also very vulnerable. As the Leader, you have to not only risk your own well-being and welfare, but the well-being and welfare of others. You hold the safety of others in your hands. One mistake could have a drastic impact on many and you will not be able to recompense them for their loss. All you will be able to do is say, "I made a mistake. I'm sorry."

As the Leader, you have to learn to believe where others fear. You have to be the voice for the voiceless, willing to speak what others are afraid to say. However, it is impossible to lead those who have let fear incapacitate them. Harriet Tubman said, "I freed a thousand slaves. I could have freed a thousand more if only they knew they were slaves."

BECOME A BI-DIMENSIONAL LEADER

What is bi-dimensional Leadership? Bi-dimensional Leadership means that you are fully present in the future, visualizing what's possible, and at the same time, you are fully present in the now, exploring ways to make it happen. As the Leader, you learn to live in both worlds at the same time. Your vision is both coming and it's here now. Therefore, you must think, believe, speak, and behave like you're already there, but work like you haven't arrived yet.

On May 25, 1961, President John F. Kennedy stood before Congress and said, "I believe that this nation should commit itself to achieving the goal, before this decade is out, of landing a man on the moon and returning him safely to the earth." Now that's bi-dimensional leadership. Only the Leader who spends time visualizing what is possible would dare to believe so boldly. As you make time to be fully present in the future (visualizing what's possible), you are also going to see these landing-on-the-moon opportunities that exist for your organization, for your department, for the city that you're leading, or even the nation that you're leading.

When I think about bi-dimensional Leaders, I think about Steve Jobs. He had this crazy idea that people were literally going to live off of their phones. Again, that is bi-dimensional leadership. He saw a future that many did not believe was possible. Steve Jobs foresaw that our entire lives would be wrapped around this little five-inch by three-inch phone. He saw that we would access email, check data and stats, search the web, and even run an entire business on a phone. This is where I want you to think like Martin Luther King Jr. Dr. King had this crazy vision. When America was segregated and very few places allowed Black people to frequent their establishments, he saw this outlandish vision that one day people are going to live together and eat together, and they would not be Black people over here and White people over there. He was a bi-dimensional Leader.

Think about Nelson Mandela. For twenty-seven years he was locked away in a prison in South Africa. After he was released, he said, "I think I'm gonna run for president now!" (My words of course). He was then elected, and this bi-dimensional Leader said, "I think I'll try to unite the entire country" (Again, my words).

What is your crazy, outlandish, landing on the moon, uniting a broken nation, creating something that no one can even comprehend vision? These great bi-dimensional Leaders did not just see what is possible, they saw themselves possible. And that is what I want for you, my friend. I want you to see all of it as possible. Why? Because you are possible.

Business advisor and author Ram Charan wrote in his book, *The Attackers Advantage*, that perceptual acuity is the ability to see beyond the bends in the road.[19] As the Leader, you must be prophetic. You must find the past, future, and present implications and trends that impact your business or your organization, your city, or even your nation, and then navigate through uncertainty to see opportunities where others see insurmountable challenges. Perceptual acuity requires you to think about how these policies and changes are going to impact your clients and how they will receive your service or your product.

I love what President Theodore Roosevelt said: "Far better to dare mighty things, to win glorious triumphs even though checkered by failure, than to rank with those poor spirits who neither

---

19 Charan, R. (2015). The Attacker's Advantage: Turning Uncertainty into Breakthrough Opportunities. Public Affairs.

enjoy nor suffer much because they live in the gray twilight that knows neither victory nor defeat."

In the book *You're It: Crisis, Change, and How to Lead When It Matters Most*, one sentence remarks, "The failure of imagination ultimately leads to the failure of leaders."[20]

COMMUNICATE A 12-MONTH S.M.A.R.T.E.S.T. VISION

McKinsey and Co. once surveyed over 2,700 Leaders on the Leader's most important job. Out of those 2,700 Leaders, 62% of them stated that the Leader's most important job or the most important Leadership behavior is communicating a clear, compelling vision that motivates and inspires[21].

Again, your most powerful force is having a clear vision. However, your most influential skill is communicating that vision so clearly that it inspires, engages, motivates, and empowers those that you lead and serve.

Here is a framework that we use within our company, BEK Impact Co., to help our clients create a clear, compelling vision that inspires, engages, motivates, and empowers those they lead and serve. If you are not clear on your vision and if you are not communicating a clear, compelling vision to your team, then your team will work with no purpose. I can say this another way: your team will always waste productivity energy, time, resources when they do not have a clear vision.

You have heard of S.M.A.R.T. Goals. S.M.A.R.T. Goals are:

---

20 Leonard J. Marcus et al., *You're it: Crisis, Change, and How to Lead When it Matters Most* (New York: PublicAffairs, 2019).
21 Keller, Scott, Meaney, Mary, and Pung, Caroline. Quarterly transformational Change Survey. McKinsey&Company January 2012.

Specific

Measurable

Attainable

Relevant

Time-bound

I have coached many organizations and many leaders on S.M.A.R.T. Goals. I have since upgraded to teaching about having a S.M.A.R.T.E.S.T. Vision. Yes. We need to have personal and organizational goals. The goal is what we are hoping to achieve. However, the S.M.A.R.T.E.S.T. Vision defines everyone's role and what it will look like, feel like, and what will be different as they pursue and achieve the goal.

There are many people who desire to increase their sales revenue. This is their goal. But it is more important for the Leader to communicate a vision of what achieving the goal looks like. A S.M.A.R.T.E.S.T. Vision helps them see how they will work, how they will work together, and the manner in which they will get things done.

It helps teams see what conversations will look like once the goal is achieved. What do they need to no longer believe once they cross the goal line? It is not just what we have to do, but what we want to see as we are doing it. This is all a part of having a S.M.A.R.T.E.S.T. Vision. You can think of a S.M.A.R.T.E.S.T. Vision as Goals 2.0.

If you really want to get people rallying around the vision, you need to create a twelve-month S.M.A.R.T.E.S.T. Vision which enables you to communicate a clear, compelling vision that inspires, engages, motivates, and empowers those whom you lead and serve. Your twelve-month S.M.A.R.T.E.S.T. Vision is not your organization's long-term, aspirational vision. This is important to have, and you must be able to let people know of an ultimate future for your organization and the people it serves. But your twelve-month S.M.A.R.T.E.S.T. Vision is your vision broken up into smaller bite-sized pieces.

I say twelve months because it is long enough to gain momentum and make shifts and changes as needed, yet short enough to keep momentum high and your team aligned and rallied around a common purpose.

So what in the world is a S.M.A.R.T.E.S.T. Vision? It is:

SPECIFIC

Your vision should be communicated with only fifteen to thirty words. You should be able to explain it in about two to three minutes. You're probably wondering, "Barry how in the world am I going to condense my vision down to fifteen to thirty words and explain it in two to three minutes?"

President John F. Kennedy stood before Congress on May 25, 1961, and stated that the US should focus on sending a man to the moon and bring him back safely to earth by the end of the decade. That is pretty specific, right? It says so much in a short, simple statement. But it also speaks to various departments and invokes curiosity in those who will be a part of it. People should understand your vision and also say, "I get it, but how in the world are we going to do that?" This is where you lay out your two-to-three-minute plan. Your explanation should tell them how you will get from point A to a successful point B.

MEASURABLE

One of the greatest gifts of your Leadership you can give is progress. People need to see and feel they are moving forward toward their S.M.A.R.T.E.S.T. Vision. This is where people see the work and risk moving them toward the vision. In order to know there is progress, you must measure the work of your people, both individually and collectively, and the resources they use to do the work.

Sales departments use sales boards to measure progress. And they also measure an individual's closing ratio to determine how many potential clients a sales person must make presentations to before they get a sale. Financial teams use budgets and ledgers to measure progress. Churches measure how many people are moving through their discipleship program and at what rate. Every Leader should have a way to measure the individual and collective performance, productivity, and quality of her team's work. The story people need to hear from you is, "When we did this, that happened, and it moved us closer to our twelve-month S.M.A.R.T.E.S.T. Vision. Let's keep getting better at it!"

ACTIONABLE

As the Leader, make sure that you have the right time, talent, and resources in place to make the S.M.A.R.T.E.S.T. Vision happen. Leaders must learn to count the cost before they implement a strategy or begin a new project. Pay attention to the capacity level of what you have and who you have in relation to where you are going and how you need to get there.

The measurement of time, talent, and resources highly impact one another. If you do not have enough time, you risk disappointing your team and wasting resources. If you do not have the right people, it will take more time and resources to achieve your S.M.A.R.T.E.S.T. Vision. And if you do not have the right resources, you will again waste time and frustrate the people.

REVOLUTIONARY

Remember I said that your job as a bi-dimensional Leader is to expose whomever you lead and serve to a future that they didn't know existed or that they didn't know they could achieve. Just like President Kennedy's vision of landing a man on the moon, you too must have a "landing on the moon" vision. Something so remarkable that it changes everything.

I do not mean you need to jeopardize or risk everything. I mean that people want Leaders who are not afraid to venture past status quo. This requires creative thinking. It requires not only looking at what is happening, but also what is not happening and why. Once you land a man on the moon, it opens the door to more discovery and possibility. Your twelve-month S.M.A.R.T.E.S.T. Vision is revolutionary when it no longer satisfies you or your team to remain where you are now.

TIME BOUND

Just as President Kennedy gave a deadline of a decade to land a man on the moon, so you must set a date by when you should achieve your twelve-month S.M.A.R.T.E.S.T. Vision. Once a deadline is set, establish a timeline. The timeline lets everyone know what must be done and by when. If you have properly considered that you have the time, talent, and resources, you will be better able to qualify a deadline and timeline (see Actionable above).

When you set a deadline, keep it. Moving the deadline lessens urgency. Leaders who constantly move deadlines lose credibility and so does the vision. People will not be as engaged if the deadline is constantly moved. People will not believe it's real until there is a deadline and a timeline attached to it. Make sure you stick with the timeline and deadline.

ENGAGING

I often say, "Vision speaks different languages at every organizational level." I have watched executive teams gather in the boardroom, discuss big ideas, and then high five each other for coming up with an awesome plan for the entire organization. It makes sense to them. It fires them up. But when they communicate it to the management team and frontline staff, it is not received as well. To them the plan is interpreted as more work, more of a burden, or "just another thing we have to work longer hours on and receive no credit!"

Make sure that your S.M.A.R.T.E.S.T. Vision speaks everyone's language. The language of your board is the bottom line. The language of your executive team is opportunity and exposure. The language of your management team is efficiency and flexibility. The language of your professional staff is efficiency, availability, and accessibility. The language of your frontline staff is simplicity and recognition. Communicate your S.M.A.R.T.E.S.T. Vision in a way that engages everyone at each level of the organization.

STRETCHES YOU

Vision must cause tension. It demands growth. It requires the breaking of old patterns. Vision cannot fit in the place you are currently in. Your current Leadership and team capacity and your organizational structure cannot contain your vision. You have to allow yourself and your teams to be stretched. Pulled. Pushed to a higher level. I know this sounds painful. But if you want to advance forward and achieve your twelve-month S.M.A.R.T.E.S.T. Vision—simply put, you have to expand your Leadership and your team's capacity.

You must be able to grow your mindset, beliefs, communication, and behaviors. As Leadership coach Marshall Goldsmith says, "What got you here won't get you there." For the sake of your twelve-month S.M.A.R.T.E.S.T. Vision, you have to get better. To get better, you must allow yourself to be stretched.

TEAM ALIGNED

A vision without alignment is anarchy. No sports team can win games if everyone does their own thing. There must be a playbook that shows how each department or each team member works together to achieve the goal. When our company is called to work with Leaders around strategy and organizational change, we often find that they are mainly focused on fixing what is broken. We help them to not just look at what needs to be fixed, but also how to align and optimize the relationship between all of the moving parts in the organization.

Your organization is a system of moving parts. No part of your organization breaks down by itself. It is the result of multiple functions of other parts. And when one part breaks down, it impacts others. So you have to be aware of how each part works together.

Don't just look at your organization as the finance department over here and R&D and marketing over there. Look at everything as one. Look into how they relate with each other. What is the relationship between the finance department and the marketing department? How does the impact of their relationship relate to the research and development department?

Your organization is like the body. The hip bone connects to the thigh bone and the thigh bone connects to the knee bone. But the function of the hip bone impacts the function of the knee bone, even though they are not directly connected. Each department in your organization is connected. It is up to you to know how they connect and lead the function of the whole, not just the parts (more on this in the next chapter).

In his book *The Four Obsessions of an Extraordinary Leader: A Leadership Fable*, Patrick Lencioni writes that the second obsession is to overcommunicate organizational clarity. As the Leader, you must continually speak the vision or the key focal point to everyone.[22] The Spirit of Leadership drives us to say yes to the vision—a clear, compelling vision. And this clear, compelling vision must be shared often.

How often do you communicate your vision to your team? Do you talk more about the work that needs to get done than the vision you are working toward? Are you the Leader that only feels successful if they do not drown and cave under the pressure? Or

---

22 Patrick Lencioni, *The Four Obsessions of an Extraordinary Leader: A Leadership Fable* (Jossey-Bass, 2000).

are you the Leader who constantly shares what is possible with your team? Communicating a clear, compelling S.M.A.R.T.E.S.T. Vision is the foundation for improving the performance, productivity, and quality of your team's work.

SEEK CLARITY AND CONVICTION

I know you've attended many conferences on clarity. You've read tons of books on clarity. And you've heard many people talk and speak on clarity. But let me tell you this: clarity is the most fundamental topic of the Leader's growth journey, and it is also one of the most overlooked.

> Clarity and conviction come from your yes to the vision, work, and risk of making things remarkably better for others.

When coaching Leaders, I tell them that they must seek clarity and conviction over certainty and consensus. Face it. You will not always know how things will turn out once you begin pursuing your twelve-month S.M.A.R.T.E.S.T. Vision. There will inevitably be bumps along the road and you will just have to learn to navigate through them. There will be times that you will not have a 100% vote in favor of moving toward your twelve-month S.M.A.R.T.E.S.T. Vision. People will object to your approach and strategy. They will group together and form a coalition to stand against what you are proposing. But the greatest achievements in history did not happen because Leaders were certain or had buy-in from everyone they led. It happened because they stood firm on their clarity and conviction.

What does it mean to seek clarity? It means that:

- You are a bi-dimensional leader.
- You have perceptual acuity; You understand the risk associated with pursuing that S.M.A.R.T.E.S.T. Vision yet you still boldly move forward toward it.
- You're not always going to be certain of the outcome but you're confident in the pursuit.
- You own that you might lose something along the way and that the journey is still worth it.
- You have searched the past, the present, and even the future trends and implications; You know what's happening around you and in your industry.

So what does it mean to seek conviction? Seeking conviction means that:

- You become one with the vision.
- Your twelve-month S.M.A.R.T.E.S.T. Vision aligns with your core beliefs and values.
- You speak up when things are working adversely against the vision that you have set.
- You listen to your instinct over the consensus of others.
- You are willing to stand alone on your decision if necessary.
- You are willing to boldly pursue this vision even if that means risking your position, your job, or even the funding.

■ You believe in it so much and you see the transformational change of others because leading transformational change is not about you; it is about the people that you lead and serve.

How many people told Patrick Bet-David that he was stupid for leaving a stable income to launch his own company? He not only launched a company. He launched a company that was in direct competition with the firm he was leaving. And this firm was one of the largest financial firms in the world. Yet Patrick did not lean on being certain. He did not worry that more were against him than for him. He stood on his clarity and conviction.

As the Leader, you must still lead with clarity and conviction. You will not be certain of the outcome. You may not always have consensus. In fact, there may be times you have to go against consensus and make decisions by clarity and conviction alone. Clarity and conviction come from your yes to the vision, work, and risk of making things remarkably better for others.

Never base your vision on what makes sense to everyone or seek consensus. Be comfortable in knowing that vision is often illogical. It was illogical for Bill Bowerman to see a waffle iron and embrace a vision of creating a shoe for runners, but nonetheless, he locked this vision in his heart and spirit and pursued his vision, using the wisdom and knowledge known to him in the moment.

And so, he and his business partner Phil Knight would later build the number one sports apparel company with the most recognizable logo in the world. You know it as Nike.

I'm sure many laughed at Bill when he told them he saw how a waffle iron could create a better sole for a shoe and that he was going to create running shoes for those in track and field. But

Bill believed in his crazy, huge vision and his belief brought a conviction and created an image in his heart to find the right information and resources to make this shoe. And as they say, the rest is history!

Do you have a crazy vision like Bill Bowerman? I hope you do because that's the vision I want to help you manifest! However, are you seeing your vision like the ten spies or like Bill and Phil? If your vision is like the ten spies, what about you makes you see so small? How is this getting in the way of what you really want to accomplish? How is this thinking hindering your team?

MAKE TIMELY, CONCISE DECISIONS

Remember, the Leader's most powerful force is having a clear, compelling vision. Also, the Leader's most influential skill is the ability to communicate a clear, compelling vision that inspires, engages, motivates, and empowers those that he leads and serves. It is also important to know that the Leader's most important job is to make concise, timely decisions. As I wrote above, you must lead with clarity and conviction. This is especially true when making decisions. Making decisions is risky. The Leader makes decisions and accepts the risks that come along with it.

I read in a *Harvard Business Review* survey that out of 2,700 Leaders, 57% of them stated that making decisions was probably the most difficult part of their job.[23] Why is making a decision the Leader's most important job and at the same time the Leader's hardest job? The answer is in the word itself. Decision. The word decision literally means to cut off. Every time you make

---

23 Carucci, Ron, Leaders, Stop Avoiding Hard Decisions, https://hbr.org/2018/04/leaders-stop-avoiding-hard-decisions (2018).

a decision, you have to cut something off. Not everything or everyone can move forward with you when you make a decision.

When you are making decisions that are going to move your organization toward your twelve-month S.M.A.R.T.E.S.T. Vision, you are not always going to be certain of the outcome. You will not have all of the information needed to make a decision. Everyone will not always agree. But you still have to make the decision with clarity and conviction.

I remember in my college economics class, I learned a term called "opportunity cost." Opportunity cost is the value of what is lost by not choosing another option. Let's say you were choosing between buying a home in the city or the rural area. You love both but have to choose one. If you choose to buy a home in the city, you lose all of the value and the lifestyle you could have had by buying a home and living in the rural area.

Here is a scenario from my favorite sport, basketball. There are .2 seconds on the clock. You have to make one shot to win the game. If you miss, you lose. You can only go by the historical data. You know who your top shooters are and who's been landing those big buckets in the last quarter. And so you decide, this is what we're going to do. You do not know if they are going to make the shot.

You do not know if someone will steal the ball on the inbound pass. You simply do not know the outcome. All you know is that this is the best plan. You know you and your team must be clear on that plan. You need to be convicted by the plan and hope that whatever they do that it works as they go and execute.

Every great Leader that has ever done something transformational in the world understands that there are old strategies and frameworks they will have to let go of once a decision is made. As Leaders, we say yes to the risk of making things remarkably better for others. Saying yes to the risk means that we will have to let go of old systems. We will have to say goodbye to old structure. People who reported to one person may now have to report to another person. And they may not be in favor of this decision. This is the risk Leaders take.

That is your role, and it's difficult. This is why not everyone can be the Leader. But guess what? You are the Leader and these are the challenges that you must accept, overcome, and even master over time.

This is all the proof you have. You will never know whether it works or not until you execute. So the outcome is really not the outcome (making the shot and winning the game). The outcome is creating and executing the best play to inbound the ball and get it into the right shooters hands, whether it works or not.

Author and business consultant Ram Charan said that taking control of uncertainty is the fundamental leadership challenge of our time.[24] It is so important that you don't practice trying to be certain, but practice being clear and convicted on the decisions that move your organization toward your twelve-month S.M.A.R.T.E.S.T. Vision.

---

24 Charan, Ram, The attacker's advantage: Turning uncertainty into breakthrough opportunities. Public Affairs. (2015).

—— CHAPTER 5 ——

LEAD THE WHOLE, NOT THE PART

Remember, your job as the Leader is to give the people you lead something to believe in. This is the vision that shows everyone a better version of themselves. It reveals better outcomes from the work they do. Once you see the vision clearly, and as your team begins to own the vision, you must learn to see and lead the whole organization, not just one department at a time.

One day a father took his four-year-old daughter to a toy store. His daughter saw a box with the picture of Elsa, Ana, and Olaf from the Disney movie, Frozen. Immediately, her eyes lit up with wonder. The daughter turned to her father and asked if he could buy it for her. She saw the picture and wanted it. It was actually a fifty-piece puzzle, but the daughter thought it was a picture she could hang on a wall in her bedroom.

When she got home, she pulled the puzzle box out of the bag and asked her father to hurry and remove all the "plastic stuff" around the box. In haste, the father removed the shrink wrap, pulled off the box top, and dumped out fifty puzzle pieces. The daughter, utterly disappointed, said to her father, "Wait a minute. This picture is broken! What happened to the picture?" She said pointing to the box cover. The father simply explained, "Sweetie, the picture is in these little broken pieces. We just have to put it together."

This is your Leadership. While others see broken pieces (how do we make all of this work?), you see the whole picture and let them know how to work to put the pieces together.

Many of our clients call us because they see the hundreds (if not thousands) of broken pieces in their organization. These broken pieces might include leading many different departments, having to make quota, balancing the budget, working with contractors, managing accounts because a worker left the company, onboarding a new executive, leading a merger, dealing with hiring shortages, and so many other organizational challenges and opportunities.

They struggle seeing how each puzzle piece connects and creates the whole picture. Or maybe, they have never known what the whole picture is supposed to be. They see scattered, broken puzzle pieces. They are not sure how to connect the pieces. Therefore, each piece is its own separate challenge.

Many Leaders base their success on how well they herd cats and put out fires. Not necessarily how well they see the whole picture, connect the pieces, and move the organization forward. They play not to lose. As long as they do not go under, they are succeeding.

The sad commentary is that too many leaders learn to adapt to just managing the broken pieces. To them, every piece is its own separate problem. Every piece needs its own solution. Every piece is separate from the other and so none of the pieces realize its individual nor corporate purpose. This is especially true in crisis situations. When something occurs that is out of the scope of standard operating procedure, people panic. But this is where the importance of having a plan comes in. Remember, without a vision, the people run wild.

If a fire breaks out in a building, there is an evacuation plan. Posted on the walls is a clear picture (the whole picture) of how everyone in the building (the individual pieces) can move cohesively (connecting the parts) to safety (all of the pieces put together). If there is an earthquake (I am from California by the way), there is a plan that tells us to drop, cover, and hold on. These plans help move many separate pieces to create a shared outcome. They are meant to create order in chaos. These plans are created to make sure every piece of the puzzle has an assignment, connects everyone together seamlessly, and achieves a corporate result. Everyone is safe. That is the whole picture.

Yes, you have many separate pieces to your puzzle. But each piece is connected to another piece. As the Leader, you have the responsibility of leading everyone toward a shared outcome. You do this by learning how each piece fits with the other, even when they operate in different departments with different operational procedures and outcomes. Create a plan that shows the whole picture and how each piece (department, team, individual, function) connects together and creates the whole picture. Help them see themselves as a part of the whole picture and not an individual puzzle piece. The whole picture is in the broken pieces.

In American football, a coach has many different players (puzzle pieces) on the field. Each player has a role to fulfill in each play. Their assignments are different. Each player must fulfill their individual assignment. It is the coach's responsibility to create a playbook that shows how each player is a part of a whole picture. Although each team member has a different assignment, they all work together to achieve the same outcome. They must each be focused on the outcome that can only be achieved by each player connecting to one another. The outcome is the whole picture.

Remember, the whole picture is in the broken pieces. The whole picture cannot be seen through one piece alone. For example, imagine the Leader discovers sales are down. This is one piece of the puzzle and a part of a larger whole picture. But the sales department is connected to other departments such as marketing, product development, R&D, and even the finance department. The Leader must be able to see how each puzzle piece connects to create the whole picture.

If sales are down, it may not always mean you need to create new incentives to increase sales or that you need a new marketing campaign. It may mean you need a new product. It could mean you need to have a crucial conversation with your sales manager. Maybe some of your sales processes need to be automated to speed up the sales cycle. It could mean your product is priced too low or too high. There are Leaders who will waste countless amounts of time, energy, and money trying to fix the one puzzle piece. When Leaders only focus on the problem and fail to see what it connects to, they miss this and make ill-informed decisions.

If your team only sees broken pieces, help them step back and see the whole picture (the outcome of what it looks like when everyone is connected and works together). This is what I mentioned in the previous chapter. The Leader gives their team a vision that they did not know could exist or did not believe was possible. Or maybe they did not know how to make it happen. So now, when they look at the broken pieces, they realize there is a whole picture in those pieces. It is easier to lead people when you can convince them of what the whole picture (when everyone is connected and works together) looks like.

Here are some thoughts to remember as you lead the whole:

- Become masterfully skilled at showing people what the picture will be once everyone is connected.
- Realize each piece has a purpose and a fit. As you have read before, know how to optimize the relationships between each individual part. Every team member, every department, and every stakeholder is holding a piece of the puzzle. It is difficult to see the full picture when no one comes together. The vision itself is a system of multiple moving pieces that must be aligned and coordinated in order to see the whole picture more clearly.
- Give people a clear, compelling vision and then inspire them to work together to manifest it (work as a team to put the puzzle pieces together).
- Be willing to adjust the vision and rearrange how things connect as the world changes around the organization.

WHY THE WHOLE MATTERS

The vision contains the connection of every part that you lead, including other contributors such as stakeholders and investors. Your current reality contains all of the individual parts. However, they may not be connected yet. It is also possible that some of the parts may need to be replaced or moved to become a fit. The whole consists of every team member working cohesively to achieve the vision. Without the whole, the vision is just a statement and is just mere words and empty rhetoric.

The vision is the picture on the box. It is what you see and what you inspire others to see. It is what you are hoping to build or establish. The whole is not necessarily the vision (the picture on the box). The whole is all of the pieces united and working collaboratively to make the vision possible. It is revealed through the connection of each team member (piece) and the relationship of their collective work and outcomes. The whole is the vision operationalized.

Those who eat at a restaurant order their food and later see the meal on the plate. However, when the chef sees the meal, he sees the ingredients and spices. He sees how he carefully measured the ingredients and spices to make sure the meal was seasoned properly. He sees the perfect temperature of the oven and the right amount of heat on the stove. He sees the cooking utensils that were used to create the meal. He sees the time it took to create the delectable delicacy. He sees the whole. The person who ordered the meal sees the final product on the plate. The chef sees everything it took to create it. And because the chef sees the whole, he is able to recreate the meal over and over again at scale.

This is why it is important for you to clearly see the vision as well as the whole. Seeing the whole helps you to answer the three questions mentioned in the "A" (Actionable) of the S.M.A.R.T.E.S.T. Vision:

1) Do we have the time?
2) Do we have the talent?
3) Do we have the resources?

Seeing the whole helps the Leader look at the organization's multiple departments, functions, and people as interrelated moving parts. In other words, each component's action causes a reaction or response within another component. Nothing operates in a vacuum. Every piece of the puzzle is only known by its connection to another piece in the puzzle. Each piece is insignificant by itself until it is connected to the rest of the pieces that reveal the picture. The accounting department cannot account for money where sales are not made. The sales department has no product or service to sell without the product development department. A product cannot be developed without a visionary.

> # Remember, as the Leader, it is your duty to lead people into a future they did not know existed or they did not believe was possible.

This works for almost any industry. Teachers cannot teach where there are no students. Doctors cannot provide quality healthcare where there are no drug manufacturing companies or healthcare equipment manufacturers.

Your ability to see the whole increases your ability to make decisions. Seeing the whole means you make decisions with the vision in mind while considering what got you to where you are now, and at the same time constantly analyzing how each individual team member will be impacted.

To see the whole the Leader must also be bi-dimensional. The Leader must be able to see what is possible for her team. She must see herself leading at a higher level. She must also realize that the vision raises the standard of everyone in the organization. The Leader must then see where the organization is now. She must see the whole picture in the scattered, unconnected pieces. Remember, as the Leader, it is your duty to lead people into a future they did not know existed or they did not believe was possible.

WORKING TO BUILD THE WHOLE

As the Leader, you now understand that everyone in your organization is connected and a part of the whole. The whole cannot manifest if people are disconnected. The whole is not each individual team member or department attempting to accomplish an individual goal. The whole is the healthy relationship between each individual team member and department, optimizing their collective impact on the goal.

One example of a business Leader who successfully brought different groups together to make a whole picture is Satya Nadella, the CEO of Microsoft. When Nadella took over the company in 2014, Microsoft was divided. There were many siloed departments and a culture of internal competition.

Nadella realized that if Microsoft was to thrive and gain the edge in the tech world, he needed to help teams see themselves as a whole and not individual parts working alone. To start connecting the parts, he implemented a series of initiatives to encourage teamwork across departments. Out of this teamwork came ideas and new innovation that many organizations now use such as cloud computing, mobile devices, and launching new collaboration products like Microsoft Teams.

But Nadella also recognized that connecting the pieces was about more than just technology and strategy. He knew that he needed to shift the company culture and identity to make all employees feel valued and heard. He introduced a new set of company values, such as "empower every person and every organization on the planet to achieve more," and began prioritizing diversity and inclusion initiatives.

Because of Nadella's Leadership, Microsoft has become a company where teams work seamlessly together, sharing resources and ideas to drive innovation and growth. The company's revenue has soared, with the cloud computing division becoming a major driver of growth. Nadella's focus on the vision and the whole has allowed Microsoft to be a leading company where both employees and customers love to be a part of.

By leading the whole, Nadella was able to transform Microsoft from a company of separate, individual pieces to connecting each piece and creating a whole, functional picture.

LEADING THE WHOLE THROUGH CHANGE

The Leader must also be aware of the shifts and turns that are occurring outside of the organization. She must—as a football term describes—learn to call an audible when necessary. The vision may need to be altered based on the economy or a shift in cultural norms. The leader who does not look into this ends up pouring resources into building something that is no longer relevant.

You have probably read many stories about how this impacted Blockbuster. They indeed had a vision of providing movie videos to consumers through video cassettes (if you were born after 2005 and do not know what video cassettes were . . . Google it!) sold in brick-and-mortar stores. The first Blockbuster store opened on October 19, 1985, in Dallas, Texas by entrepreneur David Cook. If you are like me and were born in the 70s or even before, you probably remember going to Blockbuster Video to rent a movie or two and maybe even a few video games for the weekend. We remember thousands of video cassettes and later DVDs lining the walls grouped by movie genre. You could also pick up some popcorn and snacks to go along with your movie right there in the store for your convenience. "Make it a Blockbuster Night," was their motto. You could find Blockbuster Video everywhere.

In 2004, there were 9,000 stores nationwide employing over 60,000 people. At one point Blockbuster was opening a new store every seventeen hours. It *was* a good business model. They had a vision, but they lost sight of the whole. They were so inwardly focused that they failed to focus on how people wanted to be entertained. They were no longer the gift that people wanted or needed. In 1997, Blockbuster's future competitor, Netflix, was founded. Blockbuster was known for its brick-and-mortar stores which charged customers a fee for each day they were late returning a movie rental. Blockbuster made $800 million dollars or fully 16 percent of its revenue from these late fees.

In early 2000, the founder of Netflix Reed Hastings and his partner traveled to Blockbuster's headquarters in Dallas. Hastings pitched Blockbuster on a deal to purchase his DVD-by-mail startup for $50 million, but the company decided not to make the purchase. This began the demise of Blockbuster Video. They failed to see the future of movie rental apart from their stores, late charges, and DVDs: They failed to innovate or embrace changes coming on the horizon. Part of Netflix's early success was found in adding subscribers who were tired of being charged for late returns and thus luring them away from Blockbuster.

Blockbuster began fighting back in 2004 and launched Blockbuster Online, but it was already years behind Netflix. They realized that they had to end the late fees which had been so lucrative for the company. From 2003 to 2005, the company lost 75% of its market value.[25] Netflix went on to become more popular and more profitable than Blockbuster. Hastings saw the technological and marketing opportunities to compete with Blockbuster with a subscription-by-mail DVD service. His vision, which started with a DVD subscription service, advanced to online video streaming, and then again to online streaming content creation, shows his continual willingness to innovate and embrace change. Netflix created a better business model and the whole digital phenomenon has eliminated the need for customers to go to a DVD store. Netflix and other streaming services who came after them developed a business model where subscribers enjoy unlimited rentals without late fees and without ever leaving home. The ascendance of streaming services, and Blockbuster's failure to

---

25 1. Frank Olito and Alex Bitter, "A Timeline: The Blockbuster Life Cycle," Forbes, July 11, 2012, https://www.forbes.com/2010/05/18/blockbuster-netflix-coinstar-markets-bankruptcy-coinstar_slide.html.

see the new wave until it was too late, assured the collapse of the once-successful company. In 2010, the company filed for bankruptcy and closed all its stores except for one. The one remaining Blockbuster store is in Bend, Oregon.

What happened? How did the leaders of Blockbuster miss the shift? Leaders not only take into account what is happening now, but they are also bi-dimensional. They stay ahead of the game by considering what is possible and moving toward it. The Leader looks at and allows history to inform their decisions. The Leader wants to know of similar events that have transpired in the past that might give clues as to what may happen in the present and future.

THE INDIVIDUAL AS A WHOLE

Your organization is made up of people. People do the work. Empowered, equipped, and inspired people do even greater work. But people are spiritual beings more than they are physical. Just because you see them at work does not mean they are there. Just because they nod their head in agreement in a meeting does not mean they agree. People can be in attendance and not be present.

The leader will get frustrated because he cannot figure out why people will not do what they are supposed to do or what he wants them to do. Most leaders focus on the part. They see the resume, the skills, and the accomplishments on paper. They want this kind of person to perform at the highest level. However, the leader often fails to see the other components that make up this person's being. What inspires them? What motivates them? What discourages them? If the leader only gauges performance by skill, he will miss the factors that also improve performance such as self-belief, mental toughness, and self-discipline.

The late Dr. Myles Munroe once said, "Where you get your philosophy from determines how you lead people. The way you think about people determines how you lead them or destroy them."[26]

Seeing the people you lead and serve as a whole means being fully present with them. Let's review what it means to be fully present:

> *To be so immersed in the highest future potential of others that it increases their capacity to believe for what is possible.*

A leader can easily become performance-driven. We can often unconsciously take advantage of the competency of our team and overlook who they are as people. For example, if you lead a high-performing team, it is easy to just go from goal to goal without checking in and seeing how they are doing mentally. Or you might expect the team to easily accomplish a task. Why? Because they are a high-performing team.

This may not be done intentionally, but it often happens. Leading from the Spirit of Leadership allows a leader to go from "performance" to "person." For example, my car says it can go up 180 mph. However, if I always drive at 180 mph, the engine will soon burn out. The same is true with the people you lead. Leadership begins with building the PERSON first in order to increase their PERFORMANCE. The Leader is masterful at getting the best out of people because the Leader sees the best in people.

Remember, those high-performing people you lead are first mommies and daddies managing life, household, bills, debt and school loans, relational issues, traffic and commutes, getting kids to practice, being a single parent. . . . you get it! The Leader understands that these areas can make or break their performance. So as the Leader, stay in tune with their world because their world dictates their performance. Ask, "How is this project going to impact their world and who they are (or who they feel they are) in that world?"

Leadership must be strong enough to carry the weight of who your team is becoming.

The more bureaucratic, political, or policy-driven an organization, the more connected it must be.

As Leaders, we see those we lead as a complete puzzle with all of the pieces perfectly put together. If you have ever put a jigsaw puzzle together you know that the box contains a beautiful picture of the complete puzzle. But inside the box is 100, 500, and sometimes more than 1,000 different broken pieces. Although the pieces are broken, inside those broken pieces is the full, complete picture.

Leaders are masters at putting people together. They lead from the perspective that the person is already a complete picture, and it is their job to put them together. Often, the people we lead will not know the picture. Leaders help them first see the picture, then believe the picture, and finally commit to the disciplines that bring the pieces together.

I learned five major principles about the power to engage and empower others:

1) Human beings are made to connect on a deep, spiritual level
2) The power of one's presence alone can impact another (good or bad) . . . without ever saying a word.
3) We were created to add value to people.
4) Everyone has a spirit or core of their humanity that drives their best and worst self.
5) IT'S NEVER ABOUT YOU!

The late Zig Ziglar, famed motivational speaker and author, would often say, "You can have everything in life you want, if you will just help enough other people get what they want." Remember first, people; then remember, people first. Knowing this is the beginning of leading from the Spirit of Leadership.

BECOME A SYSTEMS THINKER

Why is systems thinking important for the Spirit of Leadership? In order for things to work together, they must work together in a system. The vision, the work, and the risk of making things remarkably better for others must work seamlessly as a system. In his book, *Systems Thinking for Social Change*, my good friend David Peter Stroh wrote, "Systems thinking enables us to transform the parts of a more complex problem into a shared understanding of the larger issue, and to organize parts of a strategy into a clear direction and navigable road map."[27]

From 2017-2019, our company was contracted to work with a county education department to reduce chronic absenteeism. Chronic absenteeism is when a student misses more than 10

---

27 David Peter Stroh, *Systems Thinking for Social Change: A Practical Guide to Solving Complex Problems, Avoiding Unintended Consequences, and Achieving Lasting Results* (White River Junction, VT: Chelsea Green Publishing, 2015).

percent of the school year (in most US schools, this would be missing more than eighteen days of a 180-day school year). Their current solution was not working, and many did not know why. The vision was to implement a process that would encourage (or maybe a better word would be intimidate) parents to get their children to school on time.

Once a student was in danger of reaching the 10 percent mark, a letter would be automatically mailed to the parent first. Then, a call from the school secretary. After this, the parent would be called into the school office for a meeting where they would learn of further disciplinary efforts if they did not find a solution for getting their child to school on time. Although some tried, it was difficult to encourage a parent through punitive means.

Our team worked with five school districts. Each one followed a similar process. The challenge to all of this was everyone was focused on the absence (the individual piece) and not how the pieces connected. Many educators noticed that the letters and meetings were not working. But no one sought to change it. When we came aboard to work with these districts, we learned of many other pieces that made up the whole picture but weren't considered or looked into.

> The fact that the pieces work together to create the problem also means that the pieces must work together to create the solution.

These pieces included looking into how many students were from single-parent homes, low-income neighborhoods, and students with parents who did not have transportation and depended on public transportation to get their kids to school. Other missing pieces included school bus boundaries not extending to certain regions within the district boundaries. Therefore, the parent, who worked graveyard and did not get off until 7:30 a.m., would have to drive home, pick up their child and rush them to school only to get them there thirty minutes late.

Yet the process stayed the same. Most of these schools rarely saw the whole picture. So they attempted to fix the piece, hoping they would achieve their vision.

Trying to solve for one piece only neglected the consideration of the others. The fact that the pieces work together to create the problem also means that the pieces must work together to create the solution. It cannot be solved alone. Leading the whole means we must look at the contributing factors to both the problem and solution. Each piece is necessary and plays a role in the system.

As for the work we did with the districts on reducing chronic absenteeism, we saw the creation of a vicious cycle. Parents were told, "If you can't get your kid to school on time, we'll have to fine you." So now some parents were in a dilemma. They had to work. They had to get their kids to school on time. Some had to ask for time off work. Some had to ask neighbors. We encouraged district Leaders to look at the whole. Something as simple as helping parents create a plan that involved family members, neighbors, or other parents to help coordinate drop-offs for their child.

The same is true with the organization you lead. Has there ever been a time where you tried to fix one area of your organization, but over time saw the problem raise its ugly head in another? Or maybe you focused on fixing one problem, fixed it, but then it created another problem. If this has happened or is happening, do not worry. You are not alone. You are becoming the Leader who sees the whole.

PUTTING THE PIECES TOGETHER

I love helping my clients see the bigger picture. My objective is to help them simplify large and complex issues, especially those caused by and involving people. We send out an assessment to help them look at the problem from a macro to micro point of view. Two of the most important questions we ask are:

1) What are some of the key variables connected with the problem, and how have they been changing over time?
2) How do we (collectively and individually) contribute to the problem we are trying to solve? In particular, which of our own systems/behaviors (leadership, staff, practice, programs, services, policies, etc.) do we need to reexamine?

I want you to think about these two questions for a moment. Go back and read them again. Think about an issue you are trying to solve for your organization. Many Leaders only look to solve an issue from the place where it originated. They often overlook the contributing factors that caused the issue. But leading from the Spirit of Leadership also means you say yes to the risk of making things remarkably better for others.

Here are five steps to help you begin using a systems-thinking approach to leading the whole:

1) *Identify the root causes:* To begin the work of putting the pieces together, you have to know what is keeping the pieces disconnected. Rather than blaming one department or individuals, a systems-thinking approach involves looking into the macro context in which the problem occurs. This includes looking at organizational policies, procedures, and practices, feedback loops, and department-specific issues. By analyzing data, you can identify patterns and trends that provide clues to the root causes.

2) *Involve all stakeholders:* To lead the whole requires a collaborative effort involving all stakeholders. A systems-thinking approach involves engaging these stakeholders in identifying the root causes and co-creating solutions that are effective and sustainable. This includes using surveys, focus groups, and other forms of outreach to gather input from all stakeholders.

3) *Practice and test:* There are many proven solutions implemented by other organizations that may apply to yours. You do not have to reinvent the wheel. Evidence-based interventions reduce chronic absenteeism. These include providing positive incentives for attendance, establishing clear expectations for attendance, providing individualized support for students who are chronically absent, and addressing health-related barriers to attendance. A systems-thinking approach involves selecting interventions that are tailored to the specific needs of the school and its

students based on a comprehensive analysis of the root causes of absenteeism.

4) *Build your Leaders:* To sustain your ability to lead the whole, it is highly important to invest in Leadership development. You must nurture your team's Leadership potential. Providing Leaders with the mindset, beliefs, language, and skills needed to solve complex problems and navigate transformational change can empower them to take on greater responsibility and drive success for the organization. Prioritizing Leadership development creates a culture and identity of continuous improvement and growth where Leaders feel valued, supported, and equipped to tackle any challenge that comes their way.

5) *Monitor, evaluate, improve:* To determine the effectiveness of your strategy, you must monitor and evaluate progress regularly. Do not wait until a year or more to check if you are on track. Break down your goal into smaller goals (remember, your S.M.A.R.T.E.S.T. Vision should be measurable). This involves tracking data of everyone involved, both individually and collectively, conducting surveys and focus groups to gather feedback from stakeholders, and determining if improvements are leading to improved outcomes. A systems-thinking approach involves using data to make adjustments to strategies as needed, based on ongoing feedback and analysis.

Leading the whole requires a comprehensive and collaborative systems-thinking strategy that involves all stakeholders. By using a systems-thinking approach to identify the root causes of organizational challenges and develop strategic interventions, you can create a culture and identity where teams work cohesively to solve problems from the source in which they were derived.

—— CHAPTER 6 ——

ESTABLISH THE CULTURE AND IDENTITY

Culture. *You have read about it. You have heard speakers talk about it.* You have read books about it. And yet a strong, healthy culture remains one of the most difficult things to establish and sustain for many Leaders. But every organization has a culture. Good or bad. Love it or hate it. Your organization has a culture. You are the Chief Culture Officer. This is one Leadership responsibility that cannot be delegated. It is up to the Leader to establish, manage, maintain, model, and promote the culture. Learning how to establish your organization's culture is one topic all Leaders should be coached on. Culture can be traced to almost every organizational outcome, from how you develop your products, offer your services, and engage your community, to how you market and get paid for your services. Culture touches every part of your organization. Before you believe it is only a finance or staffing issue, step back and see what part of the culture has become dysfunctional. There is a high probability that there is an area of your culture that needs to be worked on.

> ## Culture is who I am when I am in your world. Identity is who I am because I was exposed to your world.

Peter Drucker once said that culture eats strategy for breakfast. It doesn't matter how clear or how amazing or how powerful your strategy is; if you as the Leader have not focused on developing and building the core values and the core behaviors of your organization, then your strategy, no matter how great it is, will succumb to a bad culture. To add to the late great Peter Drucker, I say, "Yes culture eats strategy for breakfast, but identity decides how much it eats." We coach our clients on creating both a healthy culture and a healthy identity. Now what is the difference between culture and identity? Here's how I define them:

Culture is who I am and what I do <u>when</u> I am with you.

Identity is who I am and what I do <u>because</u> I was with you.

Let's say you invite me and my family to your house for dinner. As we walk into your home, we notice that everyone sits at the table and eats together. However, at my house, we each fix our plate and eat wherever we want. Some are at the table while others sit on the couch and eat on a folding table so they can watch TV. But in your home, the culture is sitting and eating together at the dinner table. Whenever my family comes to your house for dinner, we assimilate into your culture.

Identity is when your culture has influenced us so much that we go back to our home, and we too begin sitting and eating together at the dinner table. It now becomes our identity. Culture is who I am when I am in your world. Identity is who I am because I was exposed to your world. People who adapt to an identity generally do so because they feel it adds value to their life.

As the Leader, you want to develop a team of directs who in turn develop their team members to own the culture, share the culture, and be the culture. This is identity. Culture and identity are a gift to those you lead and serve. The right culture and identity will empower your team for greater performance, productivity, and quality of work. If culture eats strategy for breakfast, then a healthy culture and identity can drive strategy to higher levels of change and transformation, faster.

Culture establishes a framework for how people work, how people work together, and the manner in which they get things done. This is culture. It becomes almost an obsessive demand for your organization. Identity is when your Leaders and staff begin to say, "This is how we work, this is how we work together, and this is the manner in which we get things done." They begin to own it.

Let's break this down in three steps:

1) *How people work in your organization.* If someone was working by themselves and you just so happened to observe them working, how would you want this person engaging in each step of the process? I am talking about from the receptionist to the CEO. Are they connected to the work? Are they passionate about doing the work? What draws them to want

to work at your organization? What would make them eager to come back to work the next day?

2) *How people work together in your organization.* People work harder, are more creative, and get things done faster and more efficiently when they like and have fun with the people they work with. Imagine what this would look like. What about this team collaboration would inspire greater ideas? Describe the kind of support each one would receive (especially during tough projects or when times are tough). Is there a lot of energy when teams are working? Is there a genuine appreciation of each other? Does it truly feel like a team?

Does the frontline staff feel connected to the executive team? Is the CEO or top leader friendly (not friends) with everyone? Do people feel the executive team cares about their well-being and makes decisions with their well-being in mind? Make sure you create standards for teamwork and embed the culture and identity into how people work together.

3) *How people get things done in your organization.* This is about efficiency and producing quality results. When your team has immersed themselves into the organization's identity, they want to produce something they can be proud of. Whether people are watching or not, they do not want to take short cuts. They understand that short cuts make it difficult for other departments. Think about the culture and identity of each individual, department, and team. What is the mindset, belief, language, and behavior that would drive people to want to deliver the best work, offer the best service, produce the best products, and not stop until they get

it right? What would the culture and identity look like that would make someone go above and beyond without being instructed from higher-ups?

You want your teams to assimilate into a healthy culture. You also want them to become culture carriers. These are the ones who have embraced the identity of the culture. This is important because when customers and stakeholders see your staff, they see your organization. They see you. When you receive bad service at a restaurant over and over again, you not only talk about how the server gave the worst service; you write about the restaurant's service.

Culture and identity are a powerful gift that you give to those you lead and serve. It should never be left to chance. Culture and identity are your job to create and maintain, not the job of your direct. Not anyone else. The responsibility falls on you. As I mentioned before: whether your organization is healthy, dysfunctional, or stuck . . . it ALWAYS acts like its Leader!

FIRST, TELL THE STORY

The key to building a great culture and identity is to first have a vision of what kind of culture and identity you want to establish. What organizations do you admire that have a great culture and identity? Which of these organizations seem to attract great talent, invest in their people, promote from within, and keep people for longer periods of time than other organizations? These are the organizations that most likely think about culture and identity in every aspect of their organization.

Take a look at your business process (some may call it a marketing funnel, detailing your process for customer acquisition). Think about how your organization operates from A-Z. Map out everything that needs to happen for you to make money or gain increase. For a retail store, your process might include acquiring products, marketing, selling the product, and then collecting the money. Every organization has (or must have) a simple process that clearly states how they do what they do.

Once you have your process down, begin to tell a story about how you would like the culture and identity to be as people work through each step of each process. Do not limit the possibilities. Describe how people approach the process and how collaboration is happening. Write about the attitude and behaviors you want to see throughout each step of the process.

Continue to refine the story until it feels right. Get a few team members to talk this out thoroughly. Listen to where there are differences and similarities. Then rate yourself. Don't get discouraged if you are not already doing the things you talked about in your story. This is why you are telling the story. Right now it is make-believe, but together you are making it true. At the end of the day, it's your job as the Leader to hold everyone accountable (and allow them to hold you accountable) for making this story true for your organization. The ultimate question to consider is, "How will we tie our culture and identity to our bottom line?" Your organization's culture and identity must be directly linked to improving outcomes. We will discuss this more later.

MAKE IT MATTER

If culture and identity are truly important in your organization, then it must be at the forefront of everything your organization does. It must begin with you and your Leadership team setting the example in both word and deed. It is your Leadership presence that sets the tone of your entire organization. How you show up matters. What you say and how you say it matters. How you lead in challenging times matters. I say again, whether your organization is healthy, dysfunctional, or stuck, it always acts like its Leader! You, the Leader, establish the culture of your organization. Good or bad. You guide it.

The way you make culture matter is to show it through your Leadership presence. Show up with the culture and identity. Speak through the culture and identity. Lead from the culture and identity. Whatever you define it to be, you have to be the first to immerse yourself in it. You make decisions from it. Hire from it. Promote the right team members based on it. Back it up by policy. Support it with consequences, accountability, and rewards. Let everyone know, "This is how we work, this is how we work together, and this is the manner in which we get things done!"

In a LinkedIn article written by branding and recruiting marketer, Kelli Easley, she writes about the fast food restaurant Chick-Fil-A, who hands down has one of the best cultures of all American companies. She begins her article with a story of a newly hired Chick-Fil-A executive who was beginning a presentation but was abruptly cut off by another executive leader and asked how she and her family were doing. It took her a while to realize that the company's executives had established a Culture of Care.

Easley notes that, "Leaders believe this shared kindness and connection is so key to Chick-fil-A's identity that they have shaped a corporate vision driven by care." Chick-Fil-A executives look at their "entire talent-experience lifecycle—from onboarding through development, performance management, and ways of working—to ensure it's executed in a way that is true to our brand promise."[28]

At some point, your hiring, evaluations, training, coaching, team development, and inevitably even your firing needs to move to the tempo of the culture and identity. If your organization's culture and identity is a priority, then make sure it is a part of leadership promotions and development. In the book *CEO Excellence*, Carolyn Dewar, Scott Keller, and Vikrah Malhotra call this an operating rhythm. They write, "When a CEO creates a clear and effective operating rhythm, every member of the top team can sync the rhythm of their specific area with that of the company as a whole."[29]

Every part dances in coordination with the other parts (this is a part of leading the whole as written in the previous chapter). It kind of reminds me of an orchestra. Many different instruments with different timbres. Not all play the same note. Not all play at the same time. Often, many do not even play on the same beat. But when each of them plays, they play together. You stop hearing different instruments and you only hear one melody, one unified sound. You hear the orchestra. They play in a groove.

When your team is in a groove, you will see performance, productivity, and the quality of their work improve. Leadership is

28 Kelli Easley, "Tami Piland is a self-described 'checklist person,'" LinkedIn, January 15, 2021, https://www.linkedin.com/pulse/science-care-how-chick-fil-a-systematically-built-kelli-easley/.
29 Carolyn Dewar, Scott Keller, and Vikrah Malhotra, *CEO Excellence: The Six Mindsets That Distinguish the Best Leaders from the Rest* (New York: Scribner, 2022), 141-156.

simplified when your organization has a groove. And you, Leader, are the first on the dance floor. You are the life of the party. The groove begins with you.

MAKE SURE THE CHICKEN TASTES THE SAME

I once heard a statement that said, "The chicken has to taste the same!" What in the world does this mean? In America and around the world there is a fast-food restaurant called Kentucky Fried Chicken or KFC. I heard that the chicken at KFC has the Colonel's same eleven spices and herbs in almost every KFC around the world. I heard that the chicken tastes the same.

In 2016, I visited South Africa with quite a few American peers to conduct a leadership training. After the training, we headed back to O.R. Thambo International Airport in Johannesburg. After I checked my luggage and was walking to my departure gate, I looked to my left and saw a KFC. With excitement, I said to my American peers, "Oh my gosh I have to stop and get some chicken from KFC!" My peers looked at me and said, "Barry what are you talking about? We have thousands of these in America, many right in your city. You can go to KFC when we get back to the states." I told them I had to eat KFC in South Africa because I needed to know if the chicken really tasted the same. And guess what? It actually did taste the same. Well, at least it did to me.

The chicken has to taste the same.

I want you to think about this statement as it relates to your organization. Think about the people you're leading. Think about the other departments within your organization. Be honest. Does the chicken taste the same? From the receptionist, to the frontline staff, to the supervisors and managers, and all the way to the executives and you as the Leader—does the chicken taste the same?

> # True Leaders do not focus on whether people leave them. They focus on making sure the right people stay.

Is the experience for all members of your organization consistent? Is the customer service consistent? Is the finance consistent with the marketing department? Is the marketing department consistent with the R&D department? There should be a certain seasoning and spice in your organization so that everyone who works there says, "This is how we work, this is how we work together, and this is the manner in which we get things done."

Defining your "chicken taste" (culture and identity) will cause separation in your organization. It will separate those who do not value how people work, how they work together, and the manner in which they get things done. Thus, it will also reveal those you need to let go. True Leaders do not focus on whether people leave them. They focus on making sure the right people stay.

One of the benefits of having the right chicken in your organization is that it helps to attract the right candidates and repel the wrong ones. They will look at your organization's core values and how you work, and hopefully make a conscious decision that it will not be a good fit for them. This is a good thing. It helps to weed out those who do not fit your culture and identity. It is very important that the chicken tastes the same.

Ask your team, "Does the chicken taste the same?" Work together with your team and describe the ideal, healthy culture and identity (the chicken) that must drive how you work, how you work together, and the manner in which you get things done. Consider the questions (and these questions are in no particular order):

HOW YOU WORK:

- What is your process for getting work done (must be thought out for each department as well as collectively)?
- How will your team get the most fulfillment out of their work?
- How will you make sure people are placed in the work they are most passionate about?
- Do you want A players, or will B players suffice? What would you expect from an A player?
- How will you support and hold them accountable? What will they expect from you? Who will you need to become to attract A players to do this work?
- What are some of the values that would represent their commitment to the work?
- What is their level of self-motivation and inner drive?
- What does productivity look like?
- What will make people enjoy doing the work?

- How will people be supported (trained and coached)?
- What does excellence look like (don't just say we value excellence)?
- Is Leadership modeling this?

HOW YOU WORK TOGETHER:
- What will collaboration look like (fun, creative, etc.)?
- How do we want stakeholders and customers to feel when we work with them?
- How should teams work out their differences (deal directly, respectfully, not belittling or demeaning, etc.)?
- What would need to change for frontline staff to trust upper management enough to share how they really feel?
- How will we establish trust amongst team members?
- Is Leadership modeling this?

THE MANNER IN WHICH YOU GET THINGS DONE:
- What does high-quality service look like?
- Is Leadership modeling this?
- What do we want customers to say about us?
- Can we teach this in our new employee orientation?
- How do we define our performance, productivity, and quality of work?

LINK CULTURE AND IDENTITY TO OUTCOMES

Improving your organization's culture and identity must improve outcomes. You do not just want to be voted as the best place to work. This sounds nice and it is nice to lead an organization where people love to work. But people need to know that their work matters. They want to see how their work produced outcomes. You do not just want to have a creative culture and identity. You want a creative culture and identity that brings forth creative products and services that attract the attention of potential buyers and increase market share.

You do not just want a customer-focused culture and identity. You want a customer-focused culture and identity that reduces customer attrition, customer complaints, bad press, and an inferior customer service training program. Leaders focus on creating winning environments, not just winners.

The key is to aim your culture and identity toward an outcome that would have an impact on multiple areas. Ask yourself the following:

- What is one area of our organization that, if improved, would make a drastic impact on our organization's culture and identity?
- If we are to accomplish this, what would need to change about the way we work, the way we work together, and the manner in which we get things done?

Here are a few outcomes you might see when you invest in your organization's culture and identity:

1) *Increase in Retention.* People love showing up to places where they are honored, supported, and celebrated. When this is a part of your culture and identity, you notice that your team (and clients) stick around longer.

2) *Decrease in Attrition.* As with number one, people do not quickly disconnect from organizations that make people fulfillment the main thing.

3) *Increase in Attention.* When people love their work, they pay attention to other parts that their work is connected to. They become more focused on how their work impacts the corporate outcome. They are less self-centered.

4) *Promotes Invention.* Being a part of a supportive team can bring out the best in that team. People think more clearly and are more willing to share their creative ideas.

5) *Eliminate Bad Contention.* The number one killer of team dysfunction is establishing and investing in your culture and identity. If you create and maintain a culture and identity of trust and respect, people will feel free to speak up and will release their creative ideas and not hold them back for fear of ridicule or rejection.

6) *Improve Satisfaction.* Your team might get offers from other high-profile organizations, but if you maintain a great culture and identity, it will mean more to them than higher pay from the other organization.

7) *Diverse Attraction.* If you serve a diverse group of clients or consumers, you absolutely need a diverse team. To be a diverse organization means you welcome and celebrate diverse thoughts, insights, and creative ways of getting things done.

For each of the outcomes listed above, the Leader will begin to see if there is any measurable change in how people work, how they work together, and the manner in which they get things done.

LINK CULTURE TO IDENTITY AND REWARDS

It is one thing for my wife and I to hear that our children received good grades. It is another thing to hear that our children are respectful, Leaders, exemplary students, team players, and a pleasure to have in class (all statements from their report cards). I reward them for their outcome, and I also reward them for the manner in which they achieved those outcomes. You can be an A student and not be a team player. You can have a 4.0 and not be a pleasure to have in class.

In many organizations, there are high performers who are not the best teammates. Yet leaders reward those performers who are ostracized from their team. They achieve their goal, but it is hell to work with them. What is easily missed is the fact that a great team lifts the performance of all team members. One bad team member can reduce the performance, productivity, and quality of work for others. While you think one is performing above the others, it is their caustic behavior that is undermining what other team members could produce.

The Leader who incentivizes behavior (rewarding good or ignoring bad) will tend to see more of that behavior over time. It also shows how much you value the culture and identity. If culture and identity have been tied to behavioral outcomes, then rewarding your team for displaying these behaviors will only produce greater outcomes. Think of some ways you can begin linking your organization's culture and identity to behavioral rewards.

In the book *Hidden Truths*, David Fubini talks about using psychic rewards, not just monetary rewards. Some of his ideas include:

- Assignment to lead a committee.
- Leadership of a project-based activity.
- Representing a unit of the company or the company itself to an external audience.
- Public praise.
- Invitation to address the board.
- Personal note or a call from the CEO.
- Verbal approval in a meeting.
- Invitation to go to business school for training programs.[30]

Here are a few that I have seen:

- Allowing frontline staff to weigh in on corporate decisions. Give them a seat at the table.
- Recognizing them publicly for special projects.
- Recognizing them publicly and privately for embodying the values of the company.
- Provide awards for reaching milestones (safety, years in position, years at company).
- Give them opportunities to lead special projects.
- Turn your staff appreciation days into "Oscar" like events. Have staff bring their families.

AVOID THE TYRANNY OF THE "WHAT"

One of the greatest ways to empower your team to succeed is to manage the atmosphere in which they work. Once you create the story of your culture and identity and as you begin to implement it, do everything you can to protect it. It is easy for the culture and identity to get overshadowed by politics, bureaucracy, and

---

30 Fubini, *Hidden Truths*.

the busyness of work. I once did a talk for a very large county government department in the Bay Area. The talk was entitled, *The Tyranny of the "What."* You are probably asking, "Did he mean the Tyranny of the Urgent?" No. I mean, *The Tyranny of the "What."*

What in the world is *The Tyranny of The "What?"*

The "What" is anything your organization must do to provide the product or service to the end user (your client or customer). This could include the marketing, product development, research, membership services, hiring, training, etc. The "What" contains the functions of each department that works to produce the product or service and distributing it to the end user. The "What" is the busyness of work. It is the work that absolutely has to be done in order to succeed as an organization.

In the middle of this larger circle called "What" is a smaller circle called "Who."

> Focusing on the "What"
> without the "Who" creates
> missed opportunities.

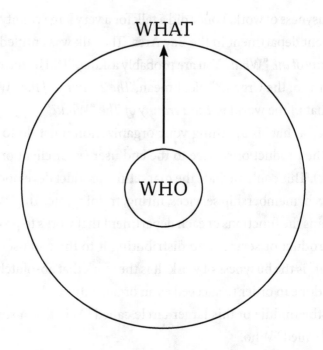

The reason why this circle in the middle is smaller than the larger circle is simply because organizations often get caught up in "What" they need to do and forget "Who" they are as an organization. This is why I call this the Tyranny of the "What." When you allow the "What" to control "Who" you are, it creates busyness. And busyness without values and purpose negatively impacts the culture and identity.

Focusing on the "What" without the "Who" creates missed opportunities. People run around like chickens with their heads cut off. When teams only operate in the "What" and fail to operate from the "Who," the "What" begins to set the tone that the work is more important than the people doing the work. This is something you absolutely need to avoid as the Leader.

"Who" your organization is will always determine what your organization is able to achieve. "Who" your organization is becomes the energy that improves how people work, how people work together, and the manner in which they get things done. It is the magic that makes people want to work for your organization or even inspires people to follow you as the Leader.

"Who" is the stuff that makes people show up early and leave late. "Who" inspires people to work harder on a project because they want the whole to win. Team members give each other high fives after a project has been completed successfully. They support each other. They are there for each other. You can see people working collaboratively because you have successfully established a strong culture and identity in your organization.

No doubt you have worked for an organization where someone was hired and literally dismantled the culture and identity of that organization within weeks. Everyone could feel that they did not fit the "Who," or the culture and identity. They did not embody the core values and disciplines. That person was hired based on what they can do. The hiring manager looked at the resume and said, "Oh my gosh! They are competent and they fit this position perfectly." Maybe they had the skills and talents that the organization needed. However, they did not fit "Who" the organization is and therefore they disrupted the culture and identity.

Leaders do not work from the "What" to the "Who," they work from the "Who" to the "What." You have to define who you are going to be as an organization. As I mentioned before, the "Who" is the energy; it is the magic that makes people want to work for your organization or even inspires people to follow you as the leader. The "Who" helps you determine the type of people that you need to hire—not just based on skill, competency, or talent—but the culture, identity, chicken, and groove of that person.

In my opinion there is one company that has successfully avoided the tyranny of the "What." No matter where you are in the world, no matter where you live, you have heard of this organization called Disney; more specifically, you've heard of Disneyland or even Disney World. This is a theme park in Anaheim, CA.

Disneyland is affectionately known as the happiest place on earth. Disneyland first focused on "Who" they are as an organization and then "What" they can do best based on who they are. One thing to note about Disneyland is that they do not have the fastest roller coasters. They do not have the roller coasters with steep ninety-degree-angle drops. If you want those kinds of rides, you'll have to find another amusement park.

Disneyland says (in my own words), "Because of our culture and identity, these are the roller coasters and rides that we will bring into our theme parks." These rides fit who they are. They want to give the people the experience that this is the happiest place on earth. So "What" they do is based on "Who" they are. Not the other way around.

As the Leader, you have to look at your organization and begin to determine what those things are that you need to do that are based on who you are as an organization. Maybe you need to restructure, you need to redefine the way you do your work, the way you work together, and the way you serve clients. Maybe you need to reformat how you create and conduct meetings, or how you develop new products and services. Maybe you need to refocus how you serve your clients and the experience they receive through your service. You need to reframe how you do what you do because in the end, you want to keep your staff inspired while working toward your S.M.A.R.T.E.S.T. Vision.

You do this by simply determining who your organization is going to be—the culture, the identity, the core principles, and the organizational character. Every aspect of Disneyland is based on who they are, which is the happiest place on earth. What is your organization based on? What is the "Who" that your organization is based on? Disneyland looks at the layout of the theme park and they base even the layout off the "Who." It is the happiest place on earth. They look at the decorations. They look at architecture. They look at every aspect, from the experience of people parking (the parking is named after their characters) to walking to the front gate. It matches who they are (their culture and identity).

When you are not investing in the culture and identity of your organization, then the quality of work will begin to decline. It will degrade, and their performance will wane if you are not investing in who your organization is.

When you work from "What" to "Who," you will notice that people start to work in silos. Teams struggle collaborating. Why? Because when the "Who" gets depleted, the "What" gets distorted! When this happens, the next thing that you will see is dysfunction creeping in and people are going to begin leaving and finding other organizations. They usually will not be leaving for higher pay, but for a better culture and identity.

You will end up with disgruntled staff if they stay on. Ultimately, disgruntled staff will produce disgruntled customers. Teams are going to eventually burn out faster. These are just a few things. I know you could probably add to this list, and I would encourage you to do so. On the flip side, what happens when you work from the "Who" to the "What?" Teams will begin collaborating more. You will solve problems faster as a team. Your leaders and team members will not be offended when they are confronted.

Maybe there is a different ideology or different opinion someone has and maybe they're going to call you out on something, but you are not offended because you understand that particular team member wants the best for you.

When you work from the "Who" to the "What," you will start seeing people assist other individuals that are not even in their department. They do this because they want a corporate win. They believe in a team win. People generally tend to stay at your organization a little longer when they enjoy the culture and identity.

Lastly, you will see teams increase productivity and performance and the quality of work. You will see greater energy because you are leading the "Who" and you are managing the "What."

KEEP YOUR HEAD ON

It is incumbent upon you to make sure that both you and your team keep your heads on. What do I mean by *"keep your head on?"* I can guarantee you that you have never been to Disneyland and seen Mickey Mouse walking around the park with his head off. You have never seen Mickey Mouse sitting on a bench taking a smoke break with his head off to the side. I absolutely know you have never seen that. How do I know this? I know this because whenever Mickey Mouse is doing his job, when he is engaged with children and adults taking pictures, Mickey Mouse is always in character. He always has his head on. This is so important as you empower people to succeed.

As the Leader, you must always keep your head on. Make sure that, even under pressure, you and everyone in the organization (including stakeholders) know how to keep your heads on. When you get frustrated in a meeting, keep your head on. When a customer complains, keep your head on. When you invest money in a project and it does not end the way you thought it should, keep your head on. Like Mickey Mouse, you, as the Lead, must always stay in character with your head on.

— CHAPTER 7 —
PRACTICE GLOBAL AWARENESS

As the Leader, you have the distinct honor of communicating a vision that cannot be seen with the natural eye and yet inspires people to believe, work, and sacrifice for it. As you learn to engage, inspire, and empower the people you lead and serve more effectively, you begin to see two worlds—yours and theirs—emerging as one.

The concept of global awareness is often associated with building stronger global partnerships to increase the awareness, demand, market share, and outcomes of a product or service that are greater than they could achieve alone. This is a very important focus for Leaders who want to expand worldwide. But in this chapter, I want to focus on how you can be more globally aware of the people you lead and serve in your organization and how this can impact your bottom line.

Here is my definition of global awareness:

The fully present state of discerning what people really need to move into a better condition of being, for themselves and the whole.

Global awareness is your ability to see beyond your team's apparent limitations and be totally immersed in their potential. Being globally aware is how you understand the culture, deep needs, experience, and mental models of the people you lead well enough to build a pathway for them to achieve the vision. The result of increasing global awareness is greater impact. The better you are at merging worlds, the better your chance of leading your organization to achieve greater success.

I have coached many leaders and their teams on engagement practices. Being globally aware seems to be the most difficult engagement practice for me to help them understand. Why? Because it is human nature to first see what is broken and not what is whole. While teaching global awareness is the most difficult, it is also the most transformative. Being globally aware silences your mental models, biases, and limited thinking about another person. You know their weaknesses, yet you see beyond that and focus on who they are called to be.

There are many Leaders who call me to coach them on how to "fix" someone's behavior. They are often hoping that I can teach them how to wave a magic wand or say a series of words to alter a team member's behavior.

A CEO once invited me to speak to about one hundred of his organization's top executives and directors. After I finished, I asked if there were any questions. One director stood up and asked me, "Barry, how do you deal with an employee who always has something negative to say in meetings and then shares her negative thoughts with others in the office? This is affecting our culture!" This employee was once his peer, but now he is her director. I simply asked the director, "What do you feel she is trying to say or accomplish by doing this?" He paused and thought for a moment about the question I had asked.

I wanted to know this because if this employee was deliberately trying to sabotage the organization's success, then he should probably let her go (or at the very least invoke some disciplinary action). The director did not feel this was the case, however. He had asked the question in front of his peers, so he had to come up with an answer. His answer was, "I don't know. I just want her to stop being negative all of the time." I empathized with the director and asked others in the room if they have ever dealt with a person like this so he would not feel alone. Many raised their hands and leaned in hoping to find a solution to their problem too. I felt there was something more to this story.

After a few follow-up questions, the director finally revealed that this employee had worked for the organization for over ten years and had been overlooked for promotion after promotion. Not because of her negativity, but because previous directors never took the time to help guide her on what she needed to work on. Over time, she became resentful which resulted in her negative attitude.

Once the director said this out loud, it was almost like the proverbial lightbulb appeared brightly over his head. I saw his own countenance light up. I then asked, "What just happened?" He became globally aware of this woman's plight. Global awareness revealed that it wasn't her negativity that was the core, it was rejection. If he settled on negativity being the problem, he would have just received more negativity from her. He would have had to fight something that was the fruit of the issue, not the root of the issue.

In this coaching moment with me, he became fully present with her plight and potential. In a moment of reflection, compassion arose within him. He put himself in her shoes and began to feel the pain of rejection she possibly has had to carry over the years. She watched other co-workers get promoted over her, even though she had been with the organization longer than them. Being globally aware was a short cut. It helped the director bypass the non-essential issues and get to the core.

The director shared that he would sit down with the employee, hear her story, determine what her career goals were, and personally coach and develop her where he could or help her get the coaching and training she needed to grow. I told the director she may come to the realization that she wants to find employment elsewhere, and that would be okay, too. The key was for him to look beyond the surface issue and drill down to find the true limits of this woman's engagement with the team and then lead her to a better condition of being, for both her and the rest of the team.

Unfortunately, I do not know the result of this encounter. I do know he did not have this solution before becoming globally aware. I know that this director felt more confident and empowered to lead this employee because he became more globally aware. He felt connected with her again and no longer felt he needed to avoid her or reprimand her for her negativity. In that moment, he no longer saw her as a problem. Her negativity diminished as his compassion grew. He became fully present in her world, understood her plight, and was able to see an opportunity he had never noticed before.

YOU ARE THEIR GUIDE

With global awareness, you become a character in their story. People join your organization with an unwritten script. The moment they are hired into your company or join your organization, you now become a part of this script. Now you must learn about their character and the role you play in their movie. In this script, you are their guide. As with most movies you have watched, you are first introduced to the main character of the movie. The writer first provides you the backstory of the main character: where they are from, who their parents are or whether they even have parents, and a glimpse of hope that they are destined to be someone great.

After this backstory, we find the character dealing with an internal and external challenge. The internal challenge is that they either do not realize how powerful they are, or they are not fully tapping into their power. The external challenge is that there is someone or something whose sole purpose is to keep them from discovering who they are or from tapping into their full power.

Over the course of the movie, we see the external antagonist controlling their life and moving them further away from their true power. Enter the guide here (think Yoda from *Star Wars*, Mickey from *Rocky Parts I, II, and III*, Shug Avery from *The Color Purple*, or Rafiki from *The Lion King*). The guide is not the main character. The guide is there for the main character. The guide is globally aware. They know the great power the main character possesses and are committed to helping them manifest it. They also know the adversity the main character faces. Even when the main character has imposed self-limitations on themselves, the guide knows who they really are and believes they have been placed in their life to help them achieve more.

> ## The Leader focuses on the person and what is possible, whereas a leader only focuses on the performance and what is missing.

The guide is globally aware enough to see how the main character can fight their way through the challenge, rise victoriously, and become a better version of themselves. In the end, the main character finally recognizes the power they possess, overcomes the antagonist, rises triumphantly, and is more prepared for the next battle (most likely a part two of the movie).

Okay. So, this is how it works in the movies. But how does this work for you as the Leader? Bottom line, you are the guide for your team. This is the presence you give to them. They join your organization with an unwritten script. They are full of potential. They have goals. They aspire to achieve those goals and even get promoted. You see great potential in them. But something keeps this individual from fulfilling their potential. Maybe they are resentful that they have been passed over for a promotion. It could be that they had high hopes for their position but realize later how difficult the job really is. There are team members who were once top producers, but life challenges caused them to drop in productivity. Through a divorce, a sick parent or child, a family death, a life-changing medical diagnosis, or a financial hardship, they soon find themselves less efficient than they once were.

When people come to work, they show up with skills, aspirations, excitement, desire, and hope, as well as fear, anxiety, worry, pain, uncertainty, regrets, and hurts. In these many different, disconnected pieces, the whole person still exists. The globally aware Leader understands human beings are complex individuals. As the Leader, you must be globally aware of what people need at the deepest level and then lead them to a better condition of being, for themselves and the whole.

Writing them up may not always be the solution. Sometimes just being the Leader who understands life happens will inspire them to show up and work better. Just like the director I mentioned earlier in this chapter, you must be globally aware to know whether you are dealing with someone who is negative or someone who feels rejected. This is not to justify keeping someone who is toxic or harmful. But it is making sure you know how to distinguish between those who are and those who are not.

The Leader focuses on the person and what is possible, whereas a leader only focuses on the performance and what is missing. The Leader also sees this person as a vital part of the whole. With you as their Leader, your team will discover gifts, talents, and skills they never knew they had. They will believe in themselves again. They will develop the experience they need to be promoted to higher levels within your organization. Some will discover their own Leadership gift and become your peer, or maybe lead another organization.

THE TEN STATES OF GLOBAL AWARENESS

Earlier you read that the Leader is bi-dimensional. The Leader is fully present in the future, visualizing what's possible, and at the same time fully present in the now, making it happen. As the Leader, you must live in both worlds at the same time. The act of "presencing" means that the future is depending on your Leadership to come into reality. Building a cohesive team, meeting goals, increasing profits, expansion, driving greater impact and change, and transforming your world are all ushered from the future to now through your Leadership.

When we blend bi-dimensional Leadership with global awareness, we not only simultaneously exist in two dimensions (future and present), but we become an observer of both dimensions as they emerge and interact together. This emerging is when you begin to speak about the vision, inspire your team to work toward it, and then begin to see improvements in your organization. This observation causes both dimensions to operate as one world. You begin to see the connection. A new world is created the moment you connect on a deeper level with the people you lead and serve.

As the globally aware Leader, it is your job to make sure this world is fruitful for all who occupy it. This is how you see the whole. It is not me and you, it is *us*. As the Leader, you create and interact in a world as one where "us" either thrives or regresses. This is what President Lincoln ultimately sought to achieve. He realized that America would never be what it was called to be with slavery as a means of demeaning and dehumanizing African slaves. America had to be one world filled with one people called Americans, of all races and ethnicities.

There are ten metaphysical states that allow the Leader to give the presence that engages, inspires, and empowers others in this new world. Being a bi-dimensional Leader is the portal into this new world. As you master these ten states, you will be better equipped to lead, coach, inspire, direct, and communicate with the people within your sphere of influence. These states allow you to observe the interaction between you and others as it is happening. Over time you will see that operating in these ten states will help you improve your engagement with others.

The Ten States of global awareness are:

1) The State of "Presencing".
2) The State of Self-Awareness.
3) The State of Mindfulness.
4) The State of Empathy.
5) The State of Active Listening.
6) The State of Curiosity.
7) The State of Love.
8) The State of Patience.
9) The State of Peace.
10) The State of Hope and Faith.

THE STATE OF "PRESENCING"

Being actively present is the first step in being globally aware. This is where you step into your role of being the guide. To do this, you must be fully present. Remember the definition of "fully present" is:

> *To be so immersed in the highest future potential of others that it increases their capacity to believe for what is possible.*

When Leaders spend time with their team, they get to know them better. They discover their greatness. And when they are in the state of "presencing," the Leader is able to earn their trust, respect, and confidence and lead them to a better state of being. The Leader sees and listens with his spirit more than his ears. He enters a room and listens to what else is in the room beyond words. Being in the state of "presencing" also requires you to be bi-dimensional. When engaging others, you must be fully present in their future while at the same time fully present in their current state, helping them to take advantage of growth opportunities.

The state of "presencing" is where the 'Aha's" and light bulb moments happen. You began to make connections between events, words, themes, and emotions. All of this leads you to communicate in a way that unlocks deeper reflection and revelation within the people you lead and serve (you will learn more about communication in the next chapter called "Speak Life").

THE STATE OF SELF-AWARENESS

In chapter two you learned that self-awareness is the ability to recognize opportunities to learn, grow, and operate more fully from the Spirit of Leadership. In this state you are constantly adjusting your belief system to stay aligned with your personal values and the optimum result that needs to take place through your interaction with others. In the state of self-awareness, you are reminded that you are a gift for the people you lead and serve. You have become their Leader and guide.

If you are with a team member and they say something that offends you, you are self-aware enough to make mental adjustments in real-time before you respond. You overcome your anger and your need to retaliate. This does not mean you allow people to run over you, or act uncharacteristically, or in a manner that interrupts organizational productivity and performance. It means you process the event differently. You maintain your dignity and honor while handling challenging people and never demean them, even if they deserve it.

Dignity and honor are the true north in the state of self-awareness. They govern your humanity and keep you centered with the human spirit. Leadership will often call for you to deal with difficult people. People will challenge you as the Leader. A team member may not always be a team player. This is a part of the risk we take of making things remarkably better for others.

Whatever the encounter, whatever the challenges you face with others, the state of self-awareness becomes a map that leads you back to the Spirit of Leadership. Even if you have to write someone up or let someone go, you do so while leaving them with their dignity and self-worth.

The result of activating self-awareness should always be personal growth and maturity. There will be times where we fail to be self-aware. Trust me, you won't always get it right. I bet you can think of a time (or two or five) where you did not handle a situation as well as you could have and, looking back now, you know you could have handled the situation in a better way. If this same situation were to occur again today, you would be more self-aware and respond in a way that leads to a better result.

As you become more globally aware, you will also notice that you become more self-aware of the biases or unprofitable mental models that keep you from learning, growing, and operating more fully in the Spirit of Leadership. The state of self-awareness becomes an alarm that alerts you to challenge your perception of another's difference so that it does not impede your ability to lead them and make things remarkably better for them.

I remember when I bought my wife a new SUV that came with a lane assist system. The lane assist system alerts the driver when the car is drifting over into another lane. Whenever the car drifts too far to the left or to the right into another lane without the turn signal on, the car automatically moves itself back between the lines of its own lane. The car is programmed to do this. This is what it is like to lead in the state of self-awareness.

When you run into challenging moments as the Leader and you feel like you are drifting into another lane, your lane assist system or being in the state of self-awareness will gently move you back into position, keeping you from any potential accidents. The state of self-awareness is a programmed mindset and belief system that keeps you driving in the lane of the Spirit of Leadership.

THE STATE OF MINDFULNESS

If "presencing" and self-awareness got together and had a baby, that baby would be named mindfulness. I can hear my mother now: "Barry, be mindful of others," or, "be mindful of your surroundings." What my mother was ultimately saying was pay attention to what is going on as it is going on. C. Otto Scharmer writes that, "Mindfulness is the capacity to pay attention to your attention."[31]

Mindfulness allows you to see yourself and those you lead and serve as individuals operating as a vital part of the same whole. It is not you and them or them and you. It is you because of them and them because of you. In the state of mindfulness, you see yourself in the meeting with your team members. You see yourself silencing your biases and prejudices and being fully present with them. You see their body language and you see yourself noticing your own body language. You see the moment you earn their trust, respect, and confidence in you. You see agreement forming.

In the state of mindfulness, you also see the connection emerging between the two of you as you are both seeking the solution. You also see new ideas and solutions being formed that could only come as a result of you both existing in this new shared world. You are in the future and present at the same time, and you are also observing the relationship between yourself and others as you actively exist in this new world. In other words, you get to see yourself and others as a better version of yourselves as you each become the whole.

Always remember, as the Leader, everything you do, every word you speak, every decision you make, and how present you are is a piece of the puzzle that creates a whole picture for everyone you lead and serve.

---

31 Scharmer, *Theory U*, 245.

To explain this more, imagine that you are in a movie where you are both actor and director. On one hand you are a character engaging with other characters, and on the other you are directing yourself. You are the performer and watching yourself perform at the same time.

THE STATE OF EMPATHY

C. Otto Scharmer wrote, "empathy allows us to see ourselves as part of a larger whole."[32] As the Leader, you are not separate from those you lead and serve. It is not you versus them.

In global awareness, there are not many cultures but one: the human culture. There are not two languages but one: the spirit language. With global awareness, the Leader seeks to find commonality, not difference. The Leader has a deep desire to expand his knowledge of the person's world in whom they are engaging. They are self-aware. They recognize opportunities to learn, grow, and operate more fully in the world occupied by the people they lead and serve. They are fully present. They are so immersed in the highest future potential of others that it increases their capacity to believe for what is possible.

THE STATE OF ACTIVE LISTENING

I have found over the years that most people who say they are good listeners are usually those who take good mental notes. They know what you said. They can almost repeat verbatim what you said. They are attentive to detail. They also listen intently so they can respond intelligibly. They do not want to respond out of context with what has been said. They believe that how they respond

---

32 Scharmer, *Theory U*, 238.

is an indication of their good listening skills. And they make sure that their response is an indication that they are listening to the person they are speaking with. Many truly want to hear what the other person is saying. However, through observation in my many trainings, about 50 percent of the attendees who say they are good listeners begin to understand that there is another level of "good" listening skills that they have not yet reached.

Level 1: Superficial listening (into your thoughts).

This level is when we listen carefully to respond articulately and intelligibly. The feelings, emotions, mental state, and experience of the person speaking to us is not the top priority. Our response to them is the top priority. So Level 1 listeners do their best to capture the data of what is being said. So Level 1 listeners do their best to capture the data of what is being said. However, they are into their own thoughts more than the deeper meaning of what a person means or feels.

As they are listening, they are determining what they feel and think about what is being said. They are looking to see whether they agree or if they have a better thought or idea to share. They are great at repeating the question or response back to the other person. They want for the people who speak to them to know that they were heard. However, Level 1 listeners often miss the heart of the matter.

Level 2: Deep listening (into their words).

The next level the Leader must achieve is listening to understand the context of one's words. The Leader is no longer into her thoughts. She is now into their words. As a person is speaking, the Leader is listening intently to the words that the other person is saying. Curiosity erupts within the Leader. As she listens, she notices how certain words reveal more of the person who is speaking. She allows their words to make connections to who they are as a whole being.

Level 3: Spirit listening (into their world)

I can remember training a group of leaders in Orange County, CA on this very subject. I gave the attendees a simple exercise to practice global awareness. The exercise was to help them move into a state of level 3 listening and then ask questions that were birthed from what they had heard by being in the state of level 3 listening (I write more on asking "presencing" questions in the next chapter). She agreed.

I simply asked Elaine, "If you could go anywhere in the world right now, where would you go?" In almost a coordinated fashion, Elaine lifted up her head and looked to the ceiling. Her body inflated with air in coordination with her head. And almost in a sigh heard by everyone in the room, as her body released pressure, she said, "Hawaii!" I then asked the other attendees to listen at the Spirit level. I encouraged them to let Elaine's response resound within their spirit. I then asked them, "Listening at a Level 3, what follow-up questions would you ask Elaine based on her response, "Hawaii?" Here are some of their responses:

"Where would you like to go when you get to Hawaii?"

"What would you want to do when you get there?"

"Sounds like you want to get away, Elaine. What type of resort would you want to stay in?"

And on and on the questions flooded in. But there was a problem. For each question Elaine's answer was simply, "I don't really know. I've never been there." I went back over the slide deck I was reviewing. I wanted them to see how global awareness is going from head to the spirit and heart. It is getting out of our own mind and being fully present in someone else's world. After they had asked as many questions as they could think of, I walked up to Elaine, looked her straight in the eyes and asked,

"Elaine, what does Hawaii mean to you right now?"

Elaine began to cry. Being globally aware of what Elaine's body language was speaking, I became curious. There was something behind her response, "Hawaii." I knew Hawaii was not a destination for her. Hawaii was relief. Hawaii was not a dream vacation for Elaine. I am sure she would have enjoyed a trip there if she could, but her response, "Hawaii," was about relief.

The room grew respectfully silent as we gave Elaine space to gather herself. After she wiped her tears, Elaine told us the story behind "Hawaii." Elaine was about sixty-four years old and retirement was nowhere in sight. On top of that, Elaine's daughter was back on drugs and left her to care for her three grandchildren. Elaine could not see a way out of the madness. She blamed herself for going back to school at a late age and not saving enough for retirement during her younger working years. Others in the room began to cry.

Look at the chart below. Take a moment a reflect on which column your listening skills fall in the most. No matter which column represents your listening skills the most, commit yourself to learning how to listen more at the Spirit level.

Superficial Listening	Deep Listening	Spirit Listening
We listen to our thoughts.	We listen to what they really mean.	We listen to what they're not saying.
We listen to how we feel about what they're saying.	We listen to how they feel about what they're saying.	We listen to the deeper meaning of what they're saying.
We listen to respond.	We listen to deliberate.	We listen to empathize.
We listen to make sure we heard them correctly.	We listen to make sure they know we heard them correctly.	We listen so they feel we understood them.
We listen to give an answer.	We listen to ask a clarifying question.	We listen to give them space to talk and process.

While you are listening, make sure the person who is speaking has your undivided attention. If you need a moment then ask them to give you a second to send the email, return a phone call, or whatever it is that may distract you from being fully present.

THE STATE OF CURIOSITY

In chapter one, I mentioned that the key to serving is paying attention. Another level of paying attention is being extremely curious. The Leader is curious, not nosy. As the Leader, you want to have an insatiable appetite to know what empowers people to succeed. Curiosity also helps you connect those separate pieces to the puzzle. It gives you insight into what the whole picture might be. The more curious you are, the better you can help lead others to life-changing discoveries for themselves and the whole.

You can change your entire organization through curiosity. Curiosity is the value that goes beyond the superficial and into the spirit of who people really are. People are not inherently lazy, mischievous, bad, or divisive. But they are hurt, broken, misguided, and abused. No, you are not their therapist. It is not your job to "fix" them or help them get healed. It is your job to lead them. Being curious, however, gives you insight into what is really happening and allows you to make better decisions, whether encouraging them to seek help or letting them go.

The opposite of curiosity is superficiality. A leader who is not curious has superficial relationships with her team. She leads a superficial organization. She makes no attempts to improve results. She only engages at the superficial level.

When practicing curiosity, you must consider:

- Their Words (what will their words reveal?).
- Their Body Language (what will their body language reveal?).
- Their Tone (what will their tone reveal?).
- Your/Their Feelings (what will their feelings reveal?).
- Your/Their mental model (what might their mental model reveal?).
- Their beliefs (what will their belief reveal?).

Leaders should listen for specific insights about what brings this person to life. The Leader who brings followers to life is the one who has her followers giving life to their organization. Creativity goes up when people are filled with life. Because you now are becoming a Level 2 and 3 listener you will be more equipped to notice significant and strategic shifts in your conversations. These shifts are the result of active listening. It is also the result of being extremely curious. A Leader is not curious because they are nosy or wish to prove a suspicion, they are curious because they sense the coachee is about to reach a breakthrough. They are curious because they sens there is something more to learn and know. They believe by listening more intently and asking a few more questions, they'll be better able to tap into the root of the true problem ans seek solutions to move past it.

Being curious is important for the Leader. As Leaders, we are always looking for that one door or path that will help us bring people into new awareness. Curiosity must always be to the benefit of the people you lead and serve. It helps you see deeper within the heart of the people you are leading.

The human spirit is the place where you feel loved, secure, and inspired. It is always the place where you worry, fear, and doubt. The Leader is in tune with these two dichotomies of the human spirit. As he is globally aware, he is sensing whether the human spirit is healed or broken, full of faith or full of doubt, uncertain or confident. He is listening beyond words.

Global awareness is about finding where the lower self is getting in the way of their Higher self. Your response is not based on opinion or what you feel is the best answer. Your response is based on noting these blockages and helping the person you lead remove them.

The more we understand the human spirit the more we can hear it speaking when no words are coming out of a person's mouth. No doubt you have asked someone, "What's wrong?"

and they answered, "Nothing." Deep down you knew something was not right. Maybe you couldn't see it, but you felt it in your core. Her spirit was crying out to your spirit for help, but her mouth couldn't articulate the need at the moment. When you are focused on profit, closing the deal, politics, or making sure everything goes your way, you miss the opportunities to engage with others on this level.

THE STATE OF LOVE

Love? Yes. Love. I am not talking about being emotionally connected with your team. I am not even talking about being more expressive to the people you lead. What I am talking about is the love for humanity and its spirit. As the Leader, you love people. You love their existence and what they have been placed on Earth to do. You love the fact that you are blessed and honored to lead them. You love that you are a part of the discovery of their Higher Self. You love that your worlds have merged into one. You love who they are becoming as they are becoming. Even when you have to let people go, you love who they are as they find their way on a new journey.

Martin Luther King, Jr. once said, "Love is the only force capable of turning an enemy to a friend."

THE STATE OF PATIENCE

I've mentioned before that it takes a lot of energy to operate in global awareness, be fully present, and do both well. Therefore, it takes practice. You will not be good at first, but over time you will be able to remain fully present for longer periods of time. When a leader has to deal with a team member, he will want to get to the point, fix the issue, and move on to the next thing. He does not have time to get to know his team members. All he wants to know is if they are producing. He is not globally aware. He is not fully present. He is not in any of the ten states of global awareness. People do not want to talk to him about issues or ideas because he is always in a state of impatience. He rushes people to get to the point and ridicules them for not knowing what he knows. This is not who you are becoming. You are the Leader who leads from the state of patience.

The Leader is careful to not project his grace on others. This is when someone expects you to be able to do something just because they can do it. The Leader understands that his experience may not always be replicated by others. Let's say two people go to the gym to lift weights. Person A weighs 165 lb. and can bench press a maximum weight of 350 lb. Person B weighs 210 lb. but can only bench press a maximum weight of 225 lb. Person A could say, "Seriously!? I weigh about 50 lb. less than you do and I can lift more weight than you!" Person A could continue to ridicule Person B for their inability to lift more weight, however, Person A would be projecting their grace on Person B unfairly. If Person A were globally aware, they would inquire with more sensitivity, learning about Person B's goals. Maybe Person B would love to lift 350 lb. one day. It could be that Person B does not have a plan on how that could be possible and would love for someone to show them how to increase their capacity to lift more weight. But if Person A simply projects their grace onto Person B, then they miss the chance to be globally aware and take an opportunity to increase the performance and productivity of Person B.

Has this ever happened to you? Have you ever wanted to increase your knowledge or performance in an area only to have a leader fuss at you because they felt you should already know how to do it? Have you ever had someone demean you just because they were faster than you or have worked in an area longer than you? If so, how did you feel when that happened? We cannot expect people to perform in the same manner we do. They will not always be attentive and respond to matters in the same way we will. Leading from the state of patience helps you to clearly see the path to help others' get where they want to go and help them overcome the roadblocks that stand in their way.

THE STATE OF PEACE

You cannot allow situations to pull you out of character. Always maintain a spirit of peace within. Chaos will ensue. You will face opposition to your plans. Some will not agree and choose to sow discord. Still maintain peace. Tap into this peace that surpasses all understanding and guards your heart and mind. Being in the state of peace does not make your situation better but it will make you better for your situation. When you are at peace you are more able to create harmony. Just as an orchestra full of instruments that perfectly blend together, as the Leader, you can bring together various gifts, talents, and temperaments to work together to create a unified outcome. You are also able to better distinguish between those tones and chords that are inharmonious.

THE STATE OF HOPE AND FAITH

Hope and faith have been so connected to religion, that it is rarely talked about in business and Leadership. But the truth of the matter is, without hope and faith, nothing you have read thus far matters. A vision can only be sustained through hope and faith. For you to be fully present is to have hope and faith. If you want to build a stronger culture and identity, you have to have hope and faith.

In the realm of Leadership, the responsibility to cultivate and radiate hope and faith rests within you. As the Leader, you hold the unique position to shape the collective mindset and belief of your team. Especially during challenging times, your unwavering commitment to being a source of hope and faith can cause a powerful ripple effect, instilling strength and resilience within each individual.

Remember, you are not only leading through directives but also through the actions that correspond with your hope and faith. By consistently demonstrating your own trust in the journey and fostering an environment of optimism, you empower your team to find solace in their shared purpose, to stay focused on the S.M.A.R.T.E.S.T. Vision, and to overcome obstacles with renewed determination.

It is natural for doubts to arise especially when faced with uncertainty. But you continue to lead with clarity and conviction, reminding your team members of the bigger picture that lies ahead.

Leading from the state of hope and faith doesn't mean denying reality. It rather involves seeing challenges as stepping stones rather than stumbling blocks. By doing this, you can help your team develop a resilient mindset that interprets difficulties as valuable lessons and essential components of the journey.

CHAPTER 8

SPEAK LIFE

Ever since I was a young child, I have loved speaking before crowds. My father was a pastor. I used to watch him rise to the platform and address the congregants in his very commanding styled voice. I watched how the people in the audience would stand on their feet, offering expressions of joy, indicating approval that his message was hitting home for them. It was early in my life that I became enamored with speaking. I can remember being about four years old and getting on stage to say my Easter and Christmas speeches at church. I was definitely dressed to impress. I may not have fully understood what my speech meant, but I was assured that I looked good and was ready to wow the crowd. I knew everyone was going to be impressed with my ability to communicate and articulate (okay, I didn't use those exact words at four years old, but you get it). I said my speech. I felt my speech. I finished my speech. And then it happened. The crowd jumped to their feet and rewarded me with a standing ovation. Now, looking back, who wouldn't cheer on a little four-year-old kid after giving a speech? You would have to be a mean-hearted, cruel human being not to!

Truth be told, I probably was not as great as I imagined. I mean, I was only four. But I knew I was confident. Over the years, as my love for speaking grew, my communication became more focused on my ability to deliver a great speech or talk. It was rarely about the people who I was speaking to. For me, the measurement of a great talk was, "How did they enjoy me?" Years later, I received opportunities to speak at conferences. These conferences had evaluations at the end. The attendees of these conferences were able to rate their satisfaction with every aspect of the conference, from the food to the location, even to the speakers and presenters. It was then that I came face-to-face with reality. I really was not as good as I thought.

After one of the conferences I spoke at, the conference host emailed me the evaluations. Each question had a Likert scale rating of 1 through 5. I started reading over the evaluations and finally came to the evaluation of the speaker. The Likert scale ratings were not that bad. Many of the ratings were a four, with a few fives, but also many threes and a small number of twos. But the kicker was when I read the open text qualitative responses. Many of the responses said something like, "The speaker was good. . . . but he talked about himself too much!" Gut punch. Hit below the belt. Ego check. I was pissed! Obviously, these people were not the best evaluators. They obviously missed how great I was. Unfortunately, I did not learn my lesson then. Thankfully, I had other chances to speak at conferences. For another speaking opportunity I had, the conference host sent me a video of my talk at my request along with the evaluations. Again, the scaled rating responses were not that bad. But then I got to the open text responses and again read the same thing as before. For some reason these people thought I talked too much about myself. Really? But now I had the video. I was going to prove them wrong.

Long story short. They were absolutely right. Dang it! I counted how many times in my talk I said "I." Yes, I made some very good points, but there was an air of arrogance as I spoke. I had not noticed this before. I made a decision right then that I did not want to be this kind of speaker any longer. But in order to become a more effective speaker I had to change my perspective of what speaking and communicating was all about.

A speaker normally stands on a stage. The lights shine and focus on the speaker while the listening audience often remains in the dark. The speaker speaks but often cannot see the people in the crowd very well because of the bright lights shining on them. This is what happens when a leader speaks. They talk and talk and talk but leave the listeners in the dark. No one really knows what to do with what they are hearing. They wonder, "*Is this person speaking to me, someone else, or themselves*?" They wonder if your talk is for them or for you.

Because the listener is in the dark, a leader speaks and cannot clearly see who he is speaking to. People move slower when they are in the dark. There is chaos when people are in the dark. Work cannot be done efficiently when people are in the dark. After a while, people stop taking risks and begin making moves to protect themselves because they are in the dark. But as the Leader, you do not speak with the light shining *on* you, you speak with the light shining *from* you.

Every time you speak, the people's faces become brighter. People see the road more clearly when you speak. Your words are light. It makes it easier to lead them to the vision when the road is well-lit. Remember, you are their guide. The purpose of your talks should bring light and revelation to the people you lead and serve. It gives new insight to the listener that they may have never thought of before. It should show them a pathway to success they have not seen before or were afraid to take before you inspired them.

As the Leader, you must be a great speaker and communicator. Whether speaking to large crowds, small groups, your team, or one-on-one, being an inspirational, influential communicator is key to empowering others to succeed. This does not mean you have to be a professional speaker like Tony Robbins, John Maxwell, or Lisa Nichols. It means you need to know how to use words that inspire people to purposeful change. This chapter is called Speak Life because I believe words can move people to believe the impossible and increase their performance, productivity, and quality of work to make it happen.

What exactly do I mean by speaking life? To speak life means:

*To communicate fluently in the language of the future
that wants to emerge and the present that calls for action.*

Speaking life gives energy, reproduces success, empowers others to grow, and helps teams respond to change. Speaking life resurrects dead things. It raises up dead hope. It brings life to dead belief. It awakens dead relationships. It invigorates dead mindsets. It brings your vision to life. Speaking life stimulates action and collaboration. It is the gift that people hold on to for years to come. Long after people move on from your Leadership, they will be able to recall and be encouraged by the words of life you spoke to them.

Speaking life is a bi-dimensional language. You speak to people's future and present. With every word, you allow their future Self to come alive in the present moment. When you speak in this manner, you will find that many people will increase their belief in themselves. Even when you correct them, you do so by speaking life.

I will never forget my elementary school principal, Mrs. Tena Petix, a White woman who led a multiethnic school. Though different in skin color than many of her students and their parents and guardians, Mrs. Petix made it her business to connect with each family on the deepest level. She had a way of speaking life to each student in her school. While I was never a kid who was called into the principal's office often, there were times when I was disciplined by Mrs. Petix. Mrs. Petix had this gift of being fully present whenever she spoke with students.

One thing she stated was that each student would thrive and be better as long as she was their principal. When she spoke to you it was evident that she only saw the greatness in you. Even when she reprimanded us as students, it was always based on reminding us of this greatness and that she was not happy when we were not living up to it. With Mrs. Petix, I never wanted to come short of what she saw in me. When she spoke life, I came alive.

This is what happens when you speak life to the people you lead and serve. They will come alive in their work. New ideas will generate more rapidly. Turnover is reduced. People love working and sacrificing for leaders who speak life.

SPEAK LIFE TO THE FUTURE AND PRESENT

Whenever there is a future that needs to emerge, there is a present that calls for action. Enter the Leader. As the Leader, you are able to help people tap into the Source of their highest future potential and inspire hope, action, and change. You get to show them a future they did not know existed or maybe did not believe was possible.

One of my favorite leaders who articulated this kind of Leadership is Dr. Martin Luther King, Jr. Let's look at how he did this in his famous, "I Have a Dream," speech:

He was fluent in the language of the future that wanted to emerge . . .

> *I have a dream that one day down in Alabama with its vicious racists, with its governor having his lips dripping with the words of interposition and nullification, one day right down in Alabama little Black boys and Black girls will be able to join hands with little White boys and White girls as sisters and brothers. I have a dream today.*[33]

He was also fluent in the language of the present that called for action . . .

> *This is our hope. This is the faith that I go back to the South with. With this faith, we will be able to hew out*

---

33 King, Martin Luther. "I Have a Dream." March on Washington for Jobs and Freedom, Aug. 28, 1963, Lincoln Memorial, Washington DC.

of the mountain of despair a stone of hope. With this faith we will be able to transform the jangling discords of our nation into a beautiful symphony of brotherhood. With this faith we will be able to work together, to pray together, to struggle together, to go to jail together, to stand up for freedom together, knowing that we will be free one day.

We can draw inspiration from so many other great Leaders who were able to speak life in dire situations. Here is General Douglas McArthur's 1962 speech to the cadets at West Point:

He was fluent in the language of the future that wanted to emerge . . .

You now face a new world—a world of change. The thrust into outer space of the satellite, spheres and missiles marked the beginning of another epoch in the long story of mankind—the chapter of the space age. . . . We deal now not with things of this world alone, but with the illimitable distances and as yet unfathomed mysteries of the universe. We are reaching out for a new and boundless frontier.

He was also fluent in the language of the present that called for change . . .

And through all this welter of change and development, your mission remains fixed, determined, inviolable—it is to win our wars. Everything else in your professional career is but corollary to this vital dedication. All other public purposes, all other public projects, all other public needs, great or small, will find others for their accomplishment; but you are the ones who are trained to fight: yours is the profession of arms—the will to win, the sure knowledge that in war there is no substitute for victory; that if you lose, the nation will be destroyed; that the very obsession of your public service must be Duty—Honor—Country.[34]

A leader's communication usually seeks to protect or promote himself. He is careful not to incriminate himself. A leader is never vulnerable with the crowd he is speaking to. A leader communicates to let people know the part he played in success. He wants people to see that if it was not for him, the organization would not be where it is. As I write this, I am thinking of a particular leader who does this often. He does not even realize the negative impact he has on the people he leads and serves. When people leave his organization, he always blames them. I was invited to speak at an event and ran into someone I knew who was once a top executive in his organization. I asked her, "What are you doing here? Are you working here now?" She proceeded to tell me why she left the former organization. She mentioned that when she put in her resignation, the leader called her and said, "I can't believe you're doing this to me. After all I've done for you, this is how you treat me?" Not once did he inquire about what led to her decision. He never even wished her well. This was not in his character to do. I know this to be true because I have sat with this leader on multiple occasions and listened to him speak for thirty minutes straight about how his executives need to do better. He spoke as a task master and rarely congratulated his team.

---

34 "Speech to West Point Cadets, May 12, 1962," MacArthur: Remember Honor Learn, https://macarthurmilwaukeeforum.com/resources/macarthurs-speech-to-west-point-cadets-may-1962/.

> ## Speaking life is not always motivational, but it is always about pushing the people you lead and serve into greater levels of success.

Leaders are great communicators. Whether you are an introvert, extrovert, or an ambivert, being an effective communicator is vital to driving transformational change in your organization. I love to speak. I would not say that I am a professional speaker, but I love inspiring people through words. Even more so, I love pushing people into their purpose by helping them see a bigger vision and believe that they are called to achieve it. I often tell people I am not a motivational speaker. I am a pusher. As the Leader, there are times when your words need to push people, not motivate them. People will not always be motivated to do what they need to do. Fear will overtake them. They will often get into their own head and allow limiting beliefs to guide them. Your job as the Leader is to speak in a way that helps them break out of being comfortable. Speaking life is not always motivational, but it is always about pushing the people you lead and serve into greater levels of success. The gift you are giving them is a fast track into their destiny.

As the Leader, it is important that you know how to communicate to your team, partners, and stakeholders. I have coached many leaders who are learning how to become more self-aware when speaking to others. It is often easier to speak out of frustration and apologize later. A leader might say, "Well they understand I get mad sometimes," or, "They know I didn't mean it like that!" Regardless of whether they forgive you or not, there is a mark that you have left on them. They will now think twice before they approach you. Make your team feel comfortable that they can come and talk to you about anything. This is where leading from the state of active listening is important. Speaking from the ten states of global awareness means you are drawing words from the Spirit of Leadership, not the spirit of anger or frustration.

Dr. King made the picture of being "Free at Last," so compelling that it sparked astronomical levels of faith and conviction in Americans of all colors and people around the world. I want you to have an explicit view of your vision. If you want buy-in to your vision, then it must include a corporate win, meaning the team benefits and not just an individual or an elite group. Learn to communicate your vision in a way that inspires your team to march with you, grow with you, come in early with you, stay late with you, take the risk with you, and achieve goals with you. And then make sure, at some point, your marching leads to victory.

USE POWER WORDS

Joel Schwartzberg, author of *Get to the Point! Sharpen Your Message and Make Your Words Matter* wrote in a *Harvard Business Review* article about how to use the right words to inspire your team[35] He

35 Joel Schwartzberg, "Find the Right Words to Inspire Your Team," *Business Communication* (blog), *Harvard Business Review*, April 13, 2021, https://hbr.org/2021/04/find-the-right-words-to-inspire-your-team.

begins by telling leaders to avoid weak words as they limit how the Leader impacts and inspires those she leads and serves. He suggests six linguistic tactics that will help Leaders more accurately and powerfully say what they mean and mean what they say:

1) *Enable vs. Allow.* Schwartzberg states, "If your effort produced a result, you actively enabled it. If you simply removed an obstacle, you merely allowed it." Enabling means you are taking a proactive approach to moving people toward the vision. Allowing means you are simply reactive. You are managing what happens to you and the organization.

2) *Prevent vs. Avoid.* As the Leader you will just have to avoid some things. Unforeseen circumstances pop up in Leadership that cause us to play whack-a-mole or be reactive to situations. But after the situation occurs, Leaders learn to prevent situations. They learn how to prepare their organization for the next emergency. They reinforce their teams to be equipped with the knowledge to grow from the past. This also shows your team that you are committed to the vision, work, and risk of making things remarkably better for others.

3) *Act vs. Address.* Your team does not just want to see you address a situation. They want you to act on it. This is the Spirit of Leadership. You take action to speak a vision that moves the team from chaos to order. You take action on doing the work necessary to higher levels of functionality. You do not just address a problem; you take action on it, even if you are not sure of the outcome. You move forward and lead as a bi-dimensional Leader.

4) *Respond vs. React*. Reacting is the result of what the problem does to us. Responding is the result of what we do to the problem. As the Leader you must make challenges a part of your strategy. Whether internal or external, Leaders know that at some point, an obstacle will arise that the Leader must navigate the organization through. This is Leadership. You may not know when the problem will arise, but you must be equipped to responds to it when it does.

5) *Overcome vs. Face*. Yes, there will be challenges that you must face. But speaking life is about empowering people to believe that they have what it takes to overcome the challenge. Let them know of the risk, and never let them forget that they are more than able to overcome it and succeed.

6) *Accomplish vs. Meet (a Goal)*. Accomplishing a goal speaks to the collective work of the team. To just meet a goal speaks to the corporate win, but not the effort and commitment of the team. Letting people know what they accomplished shows that you are paying attention to their sacrifice and all that goes into achieving a goal.

SPEAK LIFE TO THE RISK AND REWARD

Some of the greatest speeches I have heard always included some form of reality and truth of the hardship of pursuing the vision. It is not advantageous to you nor those you lead and serve to expose them to the benefits and advantages alone. You must also alert them of the risks that will be faced as you collectively seek to achieve your vision and goals. Do not try to protect your team. Protecting your team from challenges robs them of the opportunity to grow into their potential. It keeps from them opportunities to come together, test ideas together, and unite as one solid unit.

As the Leader, speak truth to the victory they are fighting for. Also, speak truth to the battle scars that are inevitable. Some think they are helping their team by withholding this truth. They are not. They are hurting their team. Giving your team the good, the bad, and the ugly will strengthen them as you pursue your vision.

Many wartime US Presidents such as Franklin Delano Roosevelt spoke of victory, but they also spoke to the challenges they would face in the pursuit of victory. When Japan bombed Pearl Harbor on December 7, 1941, Roosevelt spoke candidly before Congress the next day in a live speech to the American people. He did not hide the challenges that they faced. At no time did he pretend that things were not as bad as they seemed. Things were really bad. So Roosevelt spoke openly and candidly about the significant challenges America faced and its impact on the future of America. But he also referenced the internal resilience and power of the American people and military. He spoke about the risk and the reward. In his famous "Infamy Speech," Roosevelt said:

> *No matter how long it may take us to overcome this premeditated invasion, the American people in their righteous might will win through to absolute victory. . . . Hostilities exist. There is no blinking at the fact that our people, our territory, and our interests are in grave danger. With confidence in our armed forces, with the unbounding determination of our people, we will gain the inevitable triumph—so help us God.*[36]

---

36 "Day of Infamy Speech," Wikipedia, updated April 29, 2023, https://en.wikipedia.org/wiki/Day_of_Infamy_speech.

After his speech, Congress voted the declaration of the state of war. Three hours later, Roosevelt signed the declaration. One speech moved a nation into action. Some fought. Others prayed and believed. All held their heads higher with patriotic vigor and commitment. One speech moved a nation. It is said that the White House received many positive responses from US citizens because of Roosevelt's speech. Even with the risk of lives that would be lost in the pending war, Roosevelt inspired the people that the risk is a necessary part of achieving the reward.

Another great Leader who boldly spoke to the risk and reward was Winston Churchill in his 1940 inaugural address as Prime Minister of the United Kingdom. He said:

> We have before us many long months of toil and struggle. You ask, what is our policy? I will say, it is to wage war with all our might, with all the strength that God can give us, to wage war against a monstrous tyranny never surpassed in the dark, lamentable catalogue of human crime. You ask, what is our aim? I can answer in one word: Victory. Victory at all costs. Victory in spite of all terror. Victory however long and hard the road may be. For without victory there is no survival.[37]

What are the challenges your organization is facing now? Are you honestly sharing these challenges with your team? Or are you trying to avoid them by withholding this information? Are you talking about the problems as a hardship to the organization

---

37 Winston Churchill, "1940 Inaugural Address." First speech as Prime Minister, House of Commons, 13 May 1940.

or using power words as an opportunity to inspire your team to work together?

The Leader knows that speaking life is a gift to people. And when these people receive this gift, it empowers how they work, how they work together, and the manner in which they get things done. This gift called speaking life magnifies the collective strength of the whole, as well as the individual parts, which makes the challenge seem more manageable and conquerable.

When a CEO I worked with was hired, he spoke life to an amazing and inspirational vision. He also spoke about the difficulties of achieving that vision. The executives who were once his peers were now the people he led. He gained their respect because he understood the current issues and challenges. Yes, people need a vision, but they also need to know that you understand the challenges they face. The solace is not in a clear vision alone. Peace and solace come when people see that you see the issues, have a solid plan to navigate the issues, and will be there supporting them through every step.

Peter Andrei speaks of this in his book *How Legendary Leaders Speak*. He admonishes Leaders to:

1) Call out the elephant in the room.

2) Talk about the uncomfortable but necessary reality.

3) Challenge the familiar beliefs.

4) Expose the impending threat.[38]

Andrei also encourages Leaders to, "Describe problems with empathy, and solutions to the problems with authority." He also points out that leaders who choose not to speak life to the risk

---

38 Peter Daniel Andrei, *How Legendary Leaders Speak: 451 Proven Communication Strategies of the World's Top Leaders* (Speak for Success Press, 2020), 81.

and reward face adverse consequences. Here are his warnings to leaders who keep their teams from the brutal truth:

- Do not obscure the brutal truth or you will be obscured.
- Do not mitigate the brutal truth, or you will be mitigated.
- Do not minimize the brutal truth, or you will be minimized.[39]

ASK "PRESENCING" QUESTIONS

How a leader asks questions can make a team member feel threatened, accused, or supported and invited to explore options for a better solution. How does your team respond to your questions?

What is a "Presencing" Question? The ability to ask questions that help people tap into the Source of their highest potential and see what's possible.

There are four outcomes of asking a "presencing" question. By seeking these four outcomes you'll empower people to search for solutions instead of walling in their problems.

A "presencing" question:

1) Asks questions that reflect Level 3 listening and an understanding of the other person's perspective.

2) Asks questions that evoke discovery, insight, commitment, or action (e.g., those that challenge the other person's assumptions).

3) Asks open-ended questions that create greater clarity, possibility, or new learning.

4) Asks questions that move the other person toward what they desire, not questions that ask them to justify or look backward.

---

39 Andrei, *How Legendary Leaders Speak*, 82.

Clues that you have asked a powerful "Presencing" Question:
When a person:

- Pauses and ponders before answering.
- Says, "Hmmm, that's a good question".
- When they slowly repeat the question you just asked.
- When they have new awareness and insight into themselves and the subject being discussed.

A "Presencing" Question is NOT:

- Offensive.
- Closed-ended.
- Unrelated to the focus of the conversation.
- Past or failure-focused.
- Suggestive.
- About you.

Here are two things to remember as you learn to ask "presencing" questions:

1) "If you say it, they REJECT it. If they say it, they OWN it!"
2) "When emotions are erratically high, intelligence is severely low."

"IF YOU SAY IT..."

This statement highlights the persuasive power of ownership and the importance of active engagement in communication. When you simply tell people what to do, they might instinctively reject it. But when you ask "presencing" questions you invite them to contribute to co-creating solutions that they feel are their own. It underscores the value of creating an environment where individuals feel heard and empowered, fostering collaboration and collective ownership of shared goals.

"WHEN EMOTIONS ARE ERRATICALLY HIGH..."

There is an inverse relationship between heightened emotions and rational thinking. When emotions run rampant, they can cloud our judgment and hinder our ability to think logically and critically.

Asking the right "presencing" questions calms the spirit and causes people to think intelligibly and move toward problem-solving.

In his book *The Catalyst: How to Change Anyone's Mind*, Jonah lists two main benefits of asking questions[40]:

1) Asking questions shifts the listener's role. It is human nature for human beings to want to do the opposite of what is asked (or told) of them. We naturally want to disagree with someone who states an opinion as fact. We tend to believe there is a better way when someone states that they feel their way is the right way. Berger says that by asking questions, the Leader preoccupies the listener with a different task: "figuring out an answer to the question."

2) Asking questions also increases buy-in. When people answer your question, their answer is personalized. It is their answer. It doesn't come from you nor anyone else. When someone answers your question, they "commit to a conclusion."

---

40 Jonah Berger, *The Catalyst: How to Change Anyone's Mind* (New York: Simon & Schuster, 2020).

What statements do you normally say to the people you lead and serve? How can you turn these statements into "presencing" questions?

TRUST IS CURRENCY, A PROMISE IS CREDIT

Earlier I wrote about earning trust, respect, and confidence. People will not receive what you have to say if they do not trust you. This is why earning trust, respect, and confidence is so important. It increases performance, productivity, and quality of work. It also improves how people work, how they work together, and the manner in which they get things done. As the Leader, you must use your gift of speaking as a tool to influence people to action. However, people do not like receiving gifts from strangers or people they do not trust. Making trust connections with your team early on is of the utmost priority for Leaders. I mentioned earlier that there are three things people are always asking themselves about their Leader:

- Do I believe you?
- How will I benefit (personally and professionally) from following you?
- Can I trust you to lead me there?

Again, you must answer all three, not in words only, but also in action. Speaking life is not just about how you say it, but also the credibility you have with those you are speaking to. In everything you do and say, you are earning people's trust. Make sure you keep your account full. Never let it go into deficit.

Trust increases slowly and depletes quickly. When you make a promise, you are asking people to loan you their trust. When you ask people to follow you toward a vision, their trust is placed in an escrow account. It neither grows nor decreases. Experiencing short-term wins does not make it grow, either. It only means they will not withdraw it. But if you default on your promise and lose their trust, they will make a full withdrawal and leave you with nothing. To turn that escrow account into an investment account, you must pay them back with corporate wins. In the end, each promise fulfilled puts more of their trust into your account.

People want to follow and work with Leaders who remain confident and positive. I do not know of anyone who would follow a Leader who is always negative or unsure of himself. This is why it is important for you to immerse yourself in your vision. Start speaking your vision while you are alone. Look in the mirror and tell yourself, "We will be (add your big, God-sized vision here)!" Maybe you think this is some foolish positive confession that motivational gurus talk about. No. This is Leadership. Everything great that has ever happened in this world began with communicating a clear vision. Someone said they were going to do it and they did it.

— CHAPTER 9 —
RAISE OTHER LEADERS

I n this decade (2020-2030), there will be a good many executive transitions. Many top executive leaders will at some point make the decision to retire. COVID-19 has brought many to realize that now is the time to start enjoying their retirement and life is not promised. Many executives have had time to evaluate their body of work, their successes, and accomplishments, and see that they really have left a great legacy.

Many will have conversations with themselves and find that the only reason they are staying is because of pride or not being able to let go of what they've held onto for so long. Many executives have already set dates to retire but will be moving their dates up. Therefore, succession planning will be key, and having a cadre of leaders ready to carry on is imperative.

Establishing a Leadership culture and identity (one that purposefully empowers upward mobility) in your organization will soon expose the gifts and talents of those often overlooked.

Being the Leader means raising the Leader who will replace you. This is not something to be considered when you are about to retire or move on to another position or organization. Raising other Leaders is a major part of your job description as the Leader. Robert Iger writes in his book *The Ride of a Lifetime: Lessons Learned from 15 Years as CEO of the Walt Disney Company*:

> *At its essence, good leadership isn't about being indispensable; it's about helping others be prepared to possibly step into your shoes—giving them access to your own decision-making, identifying the skills they need to develop and helping them improve, and, as I've had to do, sometimes being honest with them about why they're not ready for the next step up*[41].

SHARE THE BURDEN OF LEADERSHIP

One of your Leadership responsibilities is to make sure there is always a team member ready to step up and lead at any given moment, whether you are a new Leader, an established Leader, or maybe at the end of your leadership journey looking to retire. At some point in your Leadership journey, you are going to have to pass along what you have developed. Some call this succession planning.

Succession planning has become more of a hot topic these days. At BEK Impact Co, I call it "Leading with the Burden." What do I mean by leading with the burden? The development of your Leaders is more than just developing them in skills or competency or knowledge and wisdom. These areas are all necessary and it is something that they need. But I want you to think about your Leadership journey. You are in a Leadership position right now because you learned how to carry the burden. In other words,

---

41 Iger, *The Ride of a Lifetime*.

you learned how to cry and keep on leading. You learned how to take hits and still stand strong. You know how to go home and not want to come back to the office, yet still show up ready to lead. You do this because you understand the burden of Leadership.

You took on the burden of moving people into a future that they did not know existed. You understand that people are depending on you to become greater, and this is the grace that we get as Leaders. Through all of the tears. Through all of the frustration, anxiety, and worries, you do not give up because you have this opportunity to lead people into this future.

The five burdens of Leadership are:

1) *Share the burden of the vision.* I have written a lot about vision. You have read about being a bi-dimensional Leader and having perceptual acuity. As the Leader, you must share the vision with your Leaders. Give them space to talk about how they see the vision. Ask them questions like, "What would you do if you were leading this organization?"

   Take note of those Leaders who understand the vision from a future perspective. They are not just boxed into the now. They, too, are bi-dimensional. They are looking at the shifts and changes that are happening in your industry and in your organization, and even in society with changing policy and federal and local and state laws.

   They are looking at the customers and clients that you are serving to make sure that the organization can be sustained in the future. This is a part of leading with the burden. You teach them how to lead with the vision.

2) *Share the burden of the corporate culture and identity.* Remember, Leaders lead from the "Who" and manage the "What." Pay close attention to those Leaders who embody the culture and identity. They live it. It is communicated in how they work, how they work with others, and the manner in which they get things done. Who in your organization embodies the culture and identity of your organization?

3) *Share the burden of Leadership responsibility.* Leaders must know how to handle the weight of the corporate vision in their respective position. If your Leaders are going to succeed you and move the organization forward and continue that twelve-month S.M.A.R.T.E.S.T. Vision long after you have moved on to another initiative, make sure that they understand the weight of being that visionary Leader. Give them some responsibility to carry out the vision.

Now I am not talking about the type of responsibility that will crush them. You want to give them parts of the vision to carry out so that they know what it feels like to lead being the visionary Leader.

4) *Share the burden of faith and hope.* One of the reasons you are leading your organization is because you are a bi-dimensional Leader. You have never been to where you are going. You have only seen it within your spirit. But there is a certain level of faith and hope that you have inside of you that says we can do this. You have looked at historical and baseline data. You know your team and what they are capable of. You know the level of pain that they can carry and how to coach them on areas of growth. All of these areas

help you to increase your faith and hope. Listen for those Leaders who speak of possibilities. As I have stated before, you want to find Leaders who have an inexplicable faith and conviction. Give them the opportunity to get others fired up and inspired to move forward.

5) *Share the burden of discipline.* You have heard the statement, "You do not rise to your vision. You fall to your disciplines." You can have a great, clear, and compelling vision. But if you do not remain disciplined, then that vision will not be reached. The disciplines are found in the way people work and the way they work together. They are also found in the way people get things done. Your Leaders must be immersed in these disciplines. These Leadership disciplines are what Leaders must do consistently and without fail in order to move the organization to its S.M.A.R.T.E.S.T. Vision. And these disciplines are non-negotiable. Just as someone who desires to lose or gain weight, there is a diet discipline and a workout discipline that one must adhere to if they desire results. It is up to you to teach and coach your Leaders on how to manage, lead, and navigate change. You have to model the discipline of leading with your head on (remember Mickey Mouse never takes his head off when he is in character).

MOVE ALONG WHILE BRINGING ALONG

A Leadership culture and identity has a way of exposing the potential of team members often overlooked.

So how do you "Move along while bringing along?"

My suggestions below will probably not be as tactical as they are philosophical, which is the reason many executive Leaders will make their decision.

If you're considering a move and are not sure who your successor should be, consider the following:

1) *Survey your team/staff/members/community.* Find out the values of Leadership they admire and what they would want to see in new Leadership. Then identify the values of Leadership that got the organization to where it is today. You want to mentor the potential new Leader on these values. In surveying your teams, you can also find who is highly respected. If hiring from within, the potential Leader must have a vision for leading his/her peers and be willing to fire them if necessary. So, they should have a high Leadership and organizational EQ. They must also have a strong commitment to furthering the organization.

2) *After you have gathered these values, have informal vision sessions with the potential Leaders.* Ask them about the vision they see for the company. Without letting them know, weigh their initial responses on how they embody the values, culture, and identity of the organization. Considering they have the Leadership capacity and acumen, if they have the natural proclivity to speak of a vision that is in line with the values, they should be considered. You should be able to look at their prior succession through the company. Ask questions that inform you of how they made decisions at each level. Find out their intentions for promoting or seeking a specific position and see whether these intentions match your values.

The potential candidate will have a vision that inspires and impacts all levels of the organization (including the board, shareholders, members, and those it serves).

3) *Assign tasks, not titles. Still not sure who should replace you?* Share some of your decision-making responsibility with them and let them feel the pain and responsibility of carrying some of your weight. Now, I don't mean something you would normally delegate, I mean something that only the executive Leader can do. You want to see how well they handle the ugliest parts of Leadership that often no one knows you endure. If they can't lead and cry . . . they are not the one! Tell them you need them to take lead on a project and that it could make or break the organization (because you make those decisions daily!). Allow them the space and opportunity to come up with their own decisions and observe how they would organize departments (finance, marketing, HR, etc.), assess risk, and their approach and strategy. If possible, allow them to implement their strategy and bear the consequences of their decision (even if it means their job). Look to how they lead from conviction and clarity over consensus and certainty. Make sure you give them a scope of time to work in (three months, six months, twelve months, etc.).

4) *MENTOR, MENTOR, MENTOR!* Your experience is your experience, but in it is wisdom, insight, and troubleshooting skills that are necessary for coaching new executives. Don't just rely on your expertise and experience but connect that potential executive to other Leaders who share the same values. Immerse them in learning opportunities that you

participate in. Let them know the nuances to your Leadership and why you do what you do. You are not having them assimilate into your personality but into your principles.

In his book *Hidden Truths*, David Fubini says,

The best mentors focus on three elements related to their mentee's careers: coaching (in its traditional sense), career guidance, and sponsorship. Coaching helps employees deal with change overtime—from the nuts and bolts of a new position to, more importantly, understanding how to assume new leadership responsibilities. In the career guidance role, mentors help younger employees recognize the tradeoffs between personal and professional goals and responsibilities, their relationship to the corporate entity, and decisions they have to make for the immediate future as well as long term. Finally, mentees benefit immensely from sponsorship. Employees with great potential can make some big mistakes or miss some promising opportunities in the early stages of their careers. In a sponsorship role, mentors can provide crucial assistance by standing up and assuring others that their mentees can be trusted to accomplish a particular task and are worth the further investment and patience that is often required to develop great talent"[42].

OVERCOME LEADERSHIP INTIMIDATION

Let's call it what it is. It's self-centered selfishness. It's when a leader believes she cannot be valuable or respected unless she is

---

42 Fubini, *Hidden Truths*, 92.

smarter than everyone else and has all the answers and best ideas. I remember being in a meeting with a few of our consultants. I was sitting listening to them correct me on a strategy I felt was best. They were giving solutions that I did not think of. In many ways, they are ten times smarter than I am. So, I became a learner.

It does not relegate my role as CEO. It enhances it because I know how to build a team. I hired them because they are smart. That makes me smart, too. And I wouldn't be where I am without them.

Leaders, I need you to be honest with yourself. Have you not promoted someone or let someone go or rejected a team member's ideas simply because you were intimidated by their knowledge, presence, or influence?

Leadership is not knowing it all. If you are trying to be smart in everything or trying to prove you are smarter than everyone else, stop it. That's insecurity. Here is where you need to be smart:

- Be smart in knowing how to select smart people to join your team.
- Be smart in giving them a vision that inspires them.
- Be smart in listening to them.
- Be smart in giving them the freedom to do their job.
- Be smart in supporting them with the resources they need to do their job.
- Be smart in building and maintaining an organizational culture and identity that empowers how they work, how they work together, and the manner in which they get things done.

- Be smart in managing the strategy and financials so that your organization grows to the next level.

BECOME A COACHING LEADER

A *Harvard Business Review* study noted that training, as a means of professional development for their leaders and staff, can increase performance up to 22 percent. However, when you add in coaching as a part of professional development on top of the training measure, you can increase the performance of your team, your leaders, or your staff by up to 88 percent.[43]

To lead from the Spirit of Leadership, it is vitally important for you to build a coaching culture and identity. The pursuit of your S.M.A.R.T.E.S.T. Vision requires you to develop this skill. Remember as you are coaching them, always show up as a gift for them. Make sure your Leadership is a gift. Make sure your communication is a gift. Remember to be self-aware, fully present, and practice global awareness.

You are here to increase their performance. You lead them so you can help the team function and collaborate and work together more cohesively. As you do that the team is going to become more endeared to you and to the vision that they are pursuing collectively. This is the power that enhances performance and productivity and brings greater quality work from everyone.

The first part of our coaching framework is to allow that team member or your direct leader to define and envision her main goal. Everyone has a part to play in achieving the S.M.A.R.T.E.S.T.

---

43 Keith Ferrazzi, "Use Your Staff Meeting for Peer-to-Peer Coaching," *Career Coaching* (blog), February 24, 2015, *Harvard Business Review,* https://hbr.org/2015/02/use-your-staff-meeting-for-peer-to-peer-coaching.

Vision. One of the questions that you can ask your team members is, "What are your department's goals that will have the greatest impact on our S.M.A.R.T.E.S.T. Vision?" You want to give them ownership and responsibility to set a goal that not only impacts their department, but the entire organization. They need to know that every single move they make as a department leader impacts not only what their team is doing, but the entire organization. Make sure they carry this burden.

> You, as the Leader, need to know where every team member is in their process of moving toward the goal that they have set.

The second part of our coaching framework is to help your leaders develop a process for moving forward and overcoming challenges. You know very well that there are going to be some unforeseen obstacles that pop up. You want them to figure out how they are going to navigate these challenges. You do not just want them to develop a plan that says, "We're going from A to B." You want to play the devil's advocate and say, "What would happen if X occurred? What would you do if policy changed in our industry, which causes us to do things in a different way?" Make sure that there is a set process in place as well as some type of contingency plan that will help them overcome unforeseen challenges when they arise.

A couple of questions that you can ask are,

"What is your process for getting there?"

"What are you going to do if X happens?"

Another question is,

"How can we support you?"

These are some of the greatest Leadership questions that will empower them, knowing that they have your full support as well as the support of their team should they get stuck and need assistance.

The third and final part of our coaching framework is to help that Leader develop action steps and firm commitments. You want to ask them questions such as,

"What is the best way to get started?"

They have their goal. They have the processes in place. But you want to help them look at all the different ways to get started and which action step will create the greatest momentum and get their team fired up, cohesively moving together toward the goal that they stated to you in the beginning.

You also want to establish commitments. You, as the Leader, need to know where every team member is in their process of moving toward the goal that they have set. You need to ask them,

"How will I know when you got there?"

"How will I know when X has been completed?"

This way, you are not emailing them every day and looking over their shoulder and making sure that they are doing it. You give them space and check in when it is close to their deadline or when the project seems to be off target.

Tony Robbins once said, "People don't leave an environment in which they feel coached and in which they know they are growing."

CONCLUSION

A s you move on from this book, remember that your Leadership is a gift to everyone you lead and serve. Give them this gift generously. Give it to them completely. Give it to them without reservation. As the Leader, be driven by the Convicting Power that moves you to say yes to the vision, work, and risk of making things remarkably better for others.

I have not written much about this Convicting Power. But as the Leader, it is necessary that you are tapped into some Higher Power, something bigger and greater than you. It is my faith in Christ that serves as my Convicting Power. My faith convicts me to honor everyone with the highest levels of respect and dignity. I do my best to leave people better after being in my presence.

Whoever or whatever is your Convicting Power that drives you to be your best Self, as long as it moves you to make things remarkably better for others, follow it.

Here are six ways the Convicting Power can help you as the Leader:

1) *Guidance and Wisdom:* The Convicting Power provides Leaders with a source of guidance and wisdom. Leaders are often faced with complex decisions and challenging situations where they will not always know the outcome. Through

this Convicting Power, Leaders can tap into a higher level of wisdom and insight that can help them navigate difficult decisions, and lead with clarity and conviction, over certainty and consensus.

2) *Values and Morality:* The Convicting Power serves as a moral compass for Leaders. It provides a framework of values and principles that guide our thoughts, beliefs, actions, and decision-making. Leaders who have a strong connection with the Convicting Power are more likely to operate with integrity, empathy, and equality. They are able to place purpose above personal gain.

3) *Humility and Humbleness:* Recognizing the Convicting Power instills a sense of humility in Leaders. It awakens you to the moments where you can learn, grow, and operate more fully from the Spirit of Leadership. It positions you to be open to diverse perspectives. This humility allows you to lead with a servant's heart. It promotes we over I.

4) *Resilience and Purpose:* Leading from the Convicting Power provides Leaders with a sense of purpose and meaning. You begin to understand your Leadership is a part of something bigger that includes the whole. Even in the toughest times, your connection to the Convicting Power enables you to persevere through difficult times, knowing that your efforts contribute to a greater purpose.

5) *Ethical Framework:* The Convicting Power represents a set of ethical principles and values that transcend personal interests. It serves as your moral compass, helping you make ethical choices and prioritize what is best for the whole. By

aligning your Leadership with the Convicting Power, you can ensure that your decisions and actions are grounded in principles that benefit the people in your organization, your industry, and even in your world.

6) *Inspiration and Motivation:* There will be times when you want to give up. No matter how great of a gift you are, there will be people who reject it or reduce its value. The Convicting Power is a source of inspiration and motivation for Leaders. It provides you with a sense of calling and a deep-rooted devotion to make a positive impact in the lives of others. This inspiration will fuel your passion, commitment, and resilience, enabling you to lead with purpose and inspire others to partner with you as you lead them toward the vision.

What is the Convicting Power that drives you? What is the Convicting Power that is driving you to say yes—not yes to the title, but yes to the vision, the work, and the risk? When everyone says, "Go this way. This is the way everyone else is going," something in you says, "No. We need to go this way." Do you lead with clarity and conviction over certainty and consensus?

What the world needs now—yes, is love sweet love (you know the song)—are Leaders who say yes. We need government Leaders, business executives, entrepreneurs, pastors and ministers, and change-makers who commit to saying yes, every day. People will think you are crazy, and you still have to say yes. People will leave you and you still must say yes. Your closest executives will feel the vision is not possible and walk away from you, and you still must say yes. You will not always have the resources to pursue it and you still must say yes. Leadership is a series of saying yes over and over again, even when you are not clear of the outcome.

What are you saying yes to right now? Are you saying yes to others' expectations of you? Are you saying yes to please the board? Are you saying yes because you do not want to lose that influential person on your team? Or are you stepping up and saying yes to the vision (here is where we're going)? Are you saying yes to the work (this is what we have to do)? And are you saying yes to the risk (This may not work out the way we hope. But we still have to do it)?

Leadership is not merely a position or title. It is a calling. It requires faith, determination, and a genuine commitment to massively impacting those you lead and serve. The result? You make things remarkably better for others.

By embracing the Spirit of Leadership and embodying its principles, we can empower people to work together and achieve what they never thought possible. We can improve how people work, how they work together, and the manner in which they get things done. We can inspire them to improve their performance, productivity, and quality of work.

We can literally change the world when we commit to these principles. As Mahatma Gandhi once said, "The difference between what we do and what we are capable of doing would suffice to solve most of the world's problems."

My hope is that you continue to lead from the Convicting Power. I pray your Leadership empowers people to succeed. Your team is waiting for you. Your family is waiting for you. Your city and nation are waiting for you. Go and serve well as you lead yourself and others to success and significance. It is your season. It is your time. Give them the gift called Leadership.

AVAIL
PODCAST

THE AVAIL PODCAST

HOSTED BY VIRGIL SIERRA